THE  Γ

7.50

LESSLIE NEWBIGIN
BISHOP IN MADRAS

The Finality of Christ

John Knox Press
Richmond, Virginia

British edition published by
SCM Press Ltd., London

American edition published by
John Knox Press, Richmond, Virginia

Standard Book Number: 8042–0555–8
Library of Congress Catalog Card Number: 69–76216
© SCM Press Ltd. 1969
Printed in Great Britain

Contents

Preface

The material here presented was originally given as the Lyman Beecher Lectures under the auspices of the Yale University Divinity School in April 1966. With some alteration it was again given as the James Reid Lectures under the auspices of the Divinity Faculty of Cambridge University. After some revision it is now offered in book form. I am deeply grateful to those who originally invited me to give these lectures, and who treated me with the greatest kindness and hospitality at the time of their delivery. Dr V. C. Samuel of Serampore College and Dr John B. Carman of Harvard University Centre for the Study of World Religions were kind enough to read through an earlier draft and to give me many penetrating and searching criticisms. I hope that I have been able to embody in the final text some at least of their insights, but they share no responsibility for the remaining weaknesses of the argument.

The final chapter is based upon reflections which were started in my mind by Dr Paul Loefler who led a series of Bible studies on Conversion for the staff of the Division of World Mission and Evangelism of the World Council of Churches at the time when I was its director. These fresh and illuminating studies have opened up many lines of discussion and I acknowledge that this part of my argument is heavily indebted to him.

I have to thank Miss Gladys Mather for most kindly and

efficiently converting my confused bundle of papers into a clean typescript for the purpose of printing.

Studdert Kennedy used to say that any real thinking arose out of a 'pain in the mind'. This very slight book arises out of the pain in the mind which is surely a necessary part of the experience of a missionary. There may have been times when a missionary was untroubled by the slightest questions about the rightness of what he was doing, but one would have to be deaf and blind to recapture that equanimity today. Among educated and intelligent people in all parts of the world there is a general feeling that the propagation of one's particular religious beliefs is an activity which hardly accords with the real needs of our shrinking planet. A missionary is a figure out of the past. Yet it seems utterly plain that a faith which loses the desire to propagate itself has already lost its life. The question, therefore, of the sense in which uniqueness and finality ought to be claimed for the Christian faith is the life-and-death question for a missionary.

It is the essential argument of these lectures that the finality of Christ is to be understood in terms of his finality for the meaning and direction of history. After hearing the lectures a friend gave me a copy of Moltmann's book, *Theology of Hope*. When I read it, I wished that I had been providentially saved from preparing the lectures before reading that book. If that had happened, the whole argument of the lectures would have been immesurably strengthened.

It is now too late for that, and the book must go as it is. I can only hope that, even if it contains nothing new, it may help some readers to continue wrestling with an issue which is surely utterly central for any believing Christian in the life of the world today.

Madras   LESSLIE NEWBIGIN
8th December 1968

I

Introduction

Is it possible for us who live in the second half of the twentieth century to use the word 'finality' in respect of Jesus Christ? There are certainly many things which make it difficult to do so, and it will help to introduce the discussion if we begin by recalling some of them.

1. There is, first of all, the overwhelming impression which science has created in us of the vastness of space and time. Our world, which was once thought to be the centre of the whole system of creation, is now seen to be an infinitesimally small speck of·dust in a universe wherein billions of worlds, separated by inconceivable distances, are forever in movement. All that we know of human history is but a moment in the life of a universe which counts time in millions of years. How absurd, then, how arrogant to think of using the word 'finality' for something that happened a few centuries ago in an obscure corner of this obscure planet. Surely the very idea is but a survival from the days when man had not begun to understand the dimensions of the universe around him!

2. There is, secondly, our commitment to the method

of science for which every tentative conclusion is but the jumping-off point for further research. A scientist who ventured to use the word 'finality' for any of his 'conclusions' would be the laughing-stock of his colleagues. The very idea of finality is simply alien to the way in which, as modern human beings, we are bound to think.

3. Thirdly, there is the fact that between us and the world in which Christianity was born and nurtured there lies the development of the science of history. We have learned to think in historical terms which were quite alien to the men who wrote the books of the Bible and the classical Christian writings. As children of our own time we are bound to recognize that every human life and every articulated body of human thought has been shaped by the particular epoch in which it occurred and shares the relativity of that epoch. It cannot be understood except against the background of its time. Its value for us can only be known by seeing its relation to its own background, much of which we have simply outgrown. This is true of that which is recorded in the Bible as much as of any other section of recorded history. To deny this is to deny the full reality of the incarnation; to accept it is to acknowledge that the finality-language of the Bible cannot be simply carried over into the twentieth century without a thorough process of interpretation.

4. Fourthly, one would have to point to the vast development of studies in the world's religions. This has shown that there are innumerable parallels in the other great religions to the belief and practices of Chris-

tians. Christianity is not something totally *sui generis*, but is one of the family of human religions. And even if the claim can be made that, among the religions, Christianity has the position of supremacy and finality, it can at once be shown that, from the point of view of the Hindu, the Buddhist or the Muslim, an equally impressive claim can be made for the finality of these faiths. Christians were not conscious of this possibility in an earlier age, because they did not mix on a level of equality with the adherents of these faiths. Today, however, the development of a truly global civilization has altered this. Christians belong with Hindus, Muslims, Buddhists and others to a common human culture in which the commonly accepted values are sought with little reference to any religious belief. It is true and important that probably the numerical majority of the human race still lives in a pre-modern kind of society, embedded almost as completely in the old sacral cultures as their ancestors were a thousand years ago. Nevertheless, the dominant culture of our modern world is a global culture within which any claim to finality by one among the world's religions seems not merely awkward, but positively illiterate.

5. Finally, there is a factor which has not been sufficiently noticed, but which seems to me of great importance to the present discussion. I refer to what must be called the acute bad conscience of western man. This is one of the most important and most neglected facts of the modern world, and it deserves more study than it has received. It is important for our subject because discussion about the finality of Jesus is often confused

by emotional arguments about the arrogance of western Christians. Since Christianity has its main centres of power and influence among the western white races, this is a factor which cannot be overlooked in sketching the background of our problem.

The modern western white man has certainly good reasons for having a bad conscience. Whatever be the exaggerations and distortions of the polemics of anti-colonialism, the fact remains that the western white man has been guilty in recent centuries of genocide, wholesale exploitation of subject peoples, the opium wars, the slave trade, the colour bar, apartheid and the use of weapons of mass destruction on civilian populations. There is plenty of material here for a bad conscience. But the situation is made more agonizing by the fact that, burdened as he is by a bad conscience, the western white man is still compelled to play a dominant role in the world. He is the leader in the process which is called (justly or otherwise) 'development'. What is called 'development' in the modern world is movement in the direction in which the western white races have moved. The western white man is therefore still compelled to play a leadership role. He is not permitted to go away into a corner and pretend that he does not exist – which is what we want to do when we have a bad conscience. In this painful situation, the typical western white man – at least in Asia – feels himself compelled to bend over backwards in order to dispel any suggestion that he claims any superiority for his traditional morals and religion. Even if he is himself a practising Christian, he is advised to avoid any overt evidence of the fact. He wants to make it clear that he is just a technical adviser who happens to have a bit of know-how, not the apostle of a better way of life.

To indicate the distance we have travelled in this respect, I shall quote a letter written by the Honourable Court of Directors of the East India Company to their agents in Madras on 25th May 1798. (The date is to be noted.) The occasion of the letter was the receipt of a communication from Madras to the effect that the Company's servants there had decided to appropriate some unspent balance for the building of what is now St Mark's church, Georgetown. After expressing their warm approval of this decision, the Directors proceeded to express the hope that 'our servants high in station will set an example to their inferiors and others of a regular attendance in public worship on the Sabbath day', and then went on: 'To preserve the ascendancy which our national character has acquired over the minds of the natives of India must ever be of importance to the maintenance of the political power we possess in the East; and we are well persuaded that this end is not to be served either by a disregard of the external observances of religion or by any assimilations to Eastern manners and opinions, but rather by retaining all the distinctions of our national principles, character, and usages. The events which have recently passed in Europe point out that the present is, least of all, the time in which irreligion should be countenanced or encouraged; for with an attachment to the religion which we profess is found to be intimately connected an attachment to our Laws and Constitution; besides which it is calculated to produce the most beneficial effects on society, – to maintain in it the peace, the subordination, and all the principles and practices on which its stability and happiness depend.'[1]

It is a far cry from this to the modern western technical adviser, sure that his technics provide the answers to human need, but anxiously deprecating any suggestion that his traditional religion is anything more than the idiosyncrasy of the part of the world from which he happens to come.

From the arrogant complacency of the merchant princes in London at the end of the eighteenth century to the anxious desire to please of the Peace Corps volunteer in the middle of the twentieth is a long road, and we have not time here to study it. Certainly there is more in it than simply the result of passing from a provincial to a global culture. The adherents of the other great religions have had this experience also, but have not reacted in the same way. I do not find among cultured Hindus or Muslims anything like the inhibition about testifying to the saving truth of their faiths which is characteristic of the cultured western white man. Arabs have at least as heavy a load of guilt in the matter of the slave trade as have Europeans, but it is not easy to see any signs of a bad conscience about it among modern Arab nationalists. Certainly the shattering effects of two world wars upon the morals of European man has much to do with the situation I am trying to describe. Beyond that one must also acknowledge a very fundamental feature of the Christian encounter with other faiths to which Tillich has drawn attention.

For a faith which finds its centre in the Cross, the encounter with other faiths has also in it the character of
judgment. The Christian who comes for the first time
into contact with the best representatives of other
faiths finds that his own Christianity is under judgment as having been untrue to the crucified and risen
Christ. There is something authentically Christian in
an attitude of humility in the presence of other faiths.
Nevertheless, what I have called the bad conscience of
modern western man is something that goes beyond
this, and is one of the important factors to be taken
account of in any discussion of the finality of Christ
in the world of today.

Bearing in mind these factors in our present cultural
situation which make it difficult to use the word 'finality' in respect of the Christian revelation, we must now
go on to ask: what is the standpoint from which we
can begin to raise this question? To be clear about one's
standpoint is important in all enquiries, but it is especially important in this one. The more one reads the liter-
ature of the inter-religious discussion, the more one is
impressed by the fact that the real decisions are made
at the beginning of the argument, not at the end. The
decisive question is the question of starting-point. It
is essential to be aware of one's own presuppositions
and to bring them – as far as possible – into the open.
If this is not done, the most elaborate arguments will
produce no meeting of the minds.

  1. One can begin the discussion from a standpoint
outside of religion. Religion may be regarded as some-

thing which arises from various psychological or socio-logical factors, and in this case the varieties of religion can be studied, classified and compared with the objec-tivity which one expects in the work of a botanist or an entomologist. The student looks at all the religions impartially from outside, being uncommitted to the beliefs of any of them. Sometimes, but not always, this is based upon a quite explicit theory of religion as illusion. John Oman classifies these theories in a three-fold way:

(*a*) theories of the Hegelian type, which regard reli-gion as a primitive or anthropomorphic form of science;

(*b*) theories of the Schleiermacher type, which re-gard religion as a product of our feelings – for example, the work of Feuerbach; and,

(*c*) theories of the Kantian type, which see religion as something which arises out of the necessity to pre-serve moral and social values – for example, the work of Durkheim. In all these cases there is an explicit theory of religion as illusion; from one or other of these stand-points religions can be classified and compared, and – *inter alia* – the claims of Christianity considered.

2. Sometimes, however, this impartial approach to all religions is to be found in writers who do not make explicit the standpoint from which they thus judge the religions. One of the oft-told tales in this discussion is the story of the King of Benares who entertained him-self and his court by putting an elephant in the midst of half-a-dozen blind men and asked them to tell him what it was. One got hold of the trunk and said it was a rope; one of the leg and said it was a tree; one of the

ear and said it was a winnowing fan – and so on. The application is obvious. Dispute about religious truth is a dispute of blind men about an elephant. All religious views are just gropings after a reality which they cannot encompass. The wise man will not take sides. What is often not noticed is that this tale implies either a stupendous claim on the part of the teller or a confession of total agnosticism. Either it implies that the teller is in the position of the king among the blind men: he knows the reality after which the religions of the world blindly grope. In that case we must ask him to share this knowledge with us, and allow us to test its claims. Or else it implies total agnosticism: the reality after which religions grope is unknowable. In that case one must observe his conduct and see whether it reveals commitments which he is not willing explicitly to acknowledge.

3. A third possible starting-point is from within one of the religions. Beginning with an explicit acknowledgment of one's own religious commitment, one can try to enter understandingly into the religious convictions of others. The real depth of this understanding will vary greatly; one must hope that with the growing contact of cultures and religions it will acquire greater depth. But – deep or shallow – every religion must in principle seek some interpretation of other religions. If it does not do so, it cannot be the point of ultimate coherence and ultimate loyalty which religion is normally understood to be for a human being or a society. It is obvious, for instance, that Hinduism has its own very highly developed interpretation of other religions,

and it classifies them in accordance with their capacity
to lead men into the experience of realization – of unity
with the ultimate ground of being through mystical
experience. From this point of view Hinduism distinguishes in all actual religions between the essential
and the peripheral, between what brings man to actual
unity with the ultimate ground of all being and that
which is tied up with the local, cultural, tribal peculiari-
ties of the people concerned. Hinduism understands
other religions in accordance with its own deepest conviction about the nature of man and of the ground of his
being. Particular names or alleged revelations lose their
importance. The essential thing is the individual spiritual experience which they exemplify or to which they
point. This Hindu point of view has become very general
in the western world, even among those who would be
surprised to learn that they were stating the Hindu
position. One might cite as a distinguished example the
following from the closing paragraph of Tillich's book
on encounter with other religions:

> In the depth of every living religion there is a point at which the
> religion itself loses its importance, and that to which it points
> breaks through its particularity, elevating it to spiritual freedom
> and with it to a vision of the spiritual presence in other ex-
> pressions of the ultimate meaning of man's existence.[2]

On this view the particular name of Jesus of Nazareth is
left behind, and one advances to 'that to which it
points'. Although written by a Christian, this sentence
expresses with precision the Vedantic view of particular
religions, and within this view it is obviously impossible
to speak of the finality of Christ.[3]

Some Christian writers, while fully acknowledging their own Christian commitment, feel that while writing of other religions they must, so to say, keep this commitment in abeyance and work with a standard of values which will be acceptable to all men of whatever faith. I may refer, for example, to the admirable book on Comparative Religion by Professor A. C. Bouquet. The spirit with which he approaches the comparison of religions is illustrated by such sentences as the following:

The author must not commit himself to any biassed assertion about the nature of the culmination point (of religious development).

It would be improper for the author to express an opinion. . . but the reader is to 'form his own judgment'.

Out of such (sympathetic and unprejudiced study of all forms of religion) must inevitably come at last some conclusions which will command as general consent as the main conclusions which have been reached regarding the physical universe.[4]

Plainly there is very great truth in the approach represented by these quotations. When one remembers how much prejudice and fanaticism has bedevilled the relations between the religions, one must unreservedly agree that a Christian in approaching other faiths must seek the greatest possible degree of objectivity, must allow the representatives of these faiths to speak for themselves, must seek as far as he can to put himself in the position of the other man, and must seek out and welcome all the common ground that exists between the religions. This must be insisted upon against all the passionate prejudice which still makes it extremely difficult to achieve in practice.

The difficulty, however, is that a committed Christian cannot leave his Christian commitment behind when he enters upon the study of other religions. The standards by which he judges, though they will seem to him objective and unprejudiced, will inevitably be shaped by his Christian commitment. If religion deals with men's ultimate commitments, then it is surely wise to recognize that a religious man does not have a point of view which transcends that commitment and which enables him to judge other religious commitments impartially.

An extremely clear statement of the standpoint from which one can engage in the study of religions is given by Gerard van der Leeuw in his phenomenology of religion. He distinguishes between the judgment of truth which must be made by theology and the 'typical phenomenological intellectual suspense' which is necessary in order to give a true account of the phenomena of religion. But he is emphatic that no real understanding of religious phenomena can be gained by standing apart from one's own religious convictions. In this field, he writes, 'any "unprejudiced" treatment is not merely impossible but positively fatal. For it prevents the investigator's complete personality becoming engaged in his task. . . The sole possible result is an "unprejudiced" – but that is only to say unintelligent – treatment governed throughout by a religious attitude which has not been scientifically clarified, and which is therefore exempt from all criticism and discussion. For "unprejudiced" investigators are usually accustomed to beginning, without further ado, with an interpretation of religion borrowed either from some liberal western European Christianity, or from the deism of the Enlightenment, or from the so-called monism of the natural sciences.' Even of the 'phenomenological intellectual suspense' which is necessary for his work, he writes that 'it is possible only in the light of one's own experience, and this can never be freed from its own religious determinateness'.[5]

The Christian who enters into this discussion must do so with the intention not only to understand and state correctly the positions which he studies, but much more to enter into the feelings and experiences which underlie them and which are not foreign to him because they are part of the one human nature which he shares with all men. He must also be penitently aware of the fact that his own grasp of Christian truth is weak and confused, and he must expect to find that it has to be corrected as the result of his encounter with the living experience of men of other faiths. But his commitment to Jesus Christ, so far from being something which he can leave behind him for the purpose of the study, is precisely his point of entry into it.

The ensuing discussion will be on the basis of this commitment. There will be no attempt to *demonstrate* the finality of Jesus. What will be attempted will be the much more modest task of exploring what it means to claim finality for him. We shall be looking at the various ways in which Christians have interpreted this finality, and trying – from within the Christian commitment – to formulate a statement of the finality of Jesus in a way that it is possible for us, as Christians of this twentieth century, to make it.

The question whether or not the standpoint which I adopt is a standpoint within one of the religions is a matter for discussion in this and the ensuing chapters. It is possible to claim that Christ is the end of all religion, and that therefore this standpoint is one outside of the religions. Certainly it implies the possibility of a negative judgment on what is called Christianity; our standpoint is not Christianity, but the revelation of God in Jesus Christ. It is therefore possible to regard this standpoint as a standpoint outside of the religions, and to see the Gospel as essentially a secular announcement. However, as a matter of fact, most of the discussion of the finality of Christ has been conducted on the assumption that this is a discussion among the religions, and with this form of the discussion we shall begin. For this purpose I shall take as the main points of reference the World Missionary Conferences from 1910 onwards, in which the relation of the Christian message to the great world religions was intensively discussed.

NOTES

1. Despatch, 25th May 1798, 51, 52, (public). Quoted in F. Penny, *The Church in Madras*, Vol. I (London 1904), p. 419.

2. Paul Tillich, *Christianity and the Encounter of the World Religions* (New York, 1963), p. 97.

3. Unless, of course, one detached the name Christ from the name Jesus, as some writers do, and used it to refer to a being which is not to be identified with Jesus of Nazareth.

4. A. C. Bouquet, *Comparative Religion* (London, 1961), pp. 306, 299, 298.

5. G. van der Leeuw, *Religion in Essence and Manifestation* (ET, London, 1938), chapter 100, paragraph 1.

II

Christianity among the Religions

The World Missionary Conference of Edinburgh 1910 (originally given the name 'Second Ecumenical Missionary Conference') is rightly regarded as an epoch-making event in modern church history. One of the reasons for its importance lies in the vast preparatory labour which went before it. Like the other sections, the section on the Christian Message was prepared for by means of a very extensive correspondence with missionaries in all parts of the world, seeking to elicit information about the present state of the non-Christian religions and about the experience of missionaries in presenting the Gospel to their adherents. The chairman of the section was D. S. Cairns of Aberdeen, who was in turn greatly influenced in his treatment of the whole matter by his intimate friend A. G. Hogg of Madras. I mention this at this point because of the great importance which Hogg's thought was to have at the Tambaram Conference a quarter of a century later.

The conclusions to which the Edinburgh Conference was led as the result of this vast labour are well expressed in the following passage from the conclusion

of the report of the Commission on the Christian
Message:

> We have thus surveyed the entire evidence which has come
> before us from the five great fields of the missionary enter-
> prise. . . There are two very notable points in that evidence
> which nay be noticed in this place. The first of these is the
> practically universal testimony that the true attitude of the
> Christian missionary to the non-Christian religions should be
> one of true understanding and, as far as possible, of sympathy.
> That there are elements in all these religions which lie outside
> the possibility of sympathy is of course recognized, and that in
> some forms of religion the evil is appalling is also clear. But
> nothing is more remarkable than the agreement that the true
> method is that of knowledge and charity, that the missionary
> should seek for the nobler elements in the non-Christian religions
> and use them as steps to higher things, that in fact all these
> religions without exception *disclose elemental needs of the human
> soul* which Christianity alone can satisfy, and that in their
> higher forms they *plainly manifest the working of the Spirit of
> God.* On all hands the merely iconoclastic attitude is condemed
> as radically unwise and unjust.
>
> But, alone with this generous recognition of all that is true
> and good in these religions, there goes also the universal and
> emphatic witness to the absoluteness of the Christian faith. . . .
> One massive conviction animates the whole evidence: that
> Jesus Christ fulfils and supersedes all other religions, and that
> the day is approaching when to Him every knee shall bow and
> every tongue confess that He is Lord to the glory of God the
> Father (pp. 267–8).

With this should be read the following words from the
speech with which Dr Robert E. Speer closed the discussion of the report in full session of the conference:

> No one of us believes that we have the whole of this truth; if
> we believe that we have the whole of the truth, that would be
> the surrender of our conviction that Christianity is the final and
> absolute religion. How is it possible for us in a small fragment

of the long corporate experiences of humanity, a few races in a mere generation of time, to claim that we have gathered all the truth of the inexhaustible religion into our own personal comprehension and experience? We know that we have not, by reason of the primary and fundamental conviction we hold of the value of Christianity. We see this also as we lay Christianity over against the non-Christian religions of the world. We discover, as we do so, truths in Christianity which we had not discerned before, or truths in a glory, in a magnitude, that we had not before imagined. The comparison does not impoverish Christianity; it does not result in our subtracting anything from the great bulk of Christian truth on which we have laid hold. It is true that from one point of view our lessons are not to be learned from the non-Christian religions but from the non-Christian races, but there is a sense in which the non-Christian religions, while they are encumbrances upon the religious life of man, are also expressions of that religious life, and as we bring our faith over against them we shall not bring back into our faith what was not in our faith before, but we shall discern what we had not discovered was there before.

This statement makes it clear that when the commission spoke of 'Christianity' it did not mean the entire body of belief and practice which has been characteristic of Christians in history, but rather the essential revelation which none of us has fully grasped and obeyed. There is a distinction here similar to that which Hendrik Kraemer made so strongly at a later point in the discussion between 'Christianity' and 'the Gospel'.

One may summarize the position of the Edinburgh meeting in the following propositions:

1. Christianity (in the sense indicated above) is absolute. 'Jesus Christ fulfils and supersedes all other religions.'

2. It is our duty as Christians to seek out the nobler elements in other religions, and use them as stepping-

stones by which the adherents of those religions may be led to higher things.

3. All religions disclose needs of the human soul which Jesus alone can satisfy.

4. The higher forms of the non-Christian religions manifest the working of the Holy Spirit.

5. Christianity (understood here as empirical, historic Christianity, not in the sense of proposition 1 above) is enriched by treasures from the other religions through sympathetic contact between Christians and men of other faiths.

These propositions clearly raise the following questions, among others :

1. In what sense does Jesus fulfil the other religions? Is it only that he satisfies needs which other religions manifest but cannot satisfy? Or does he in some sense complete that which they have only in part? Is it possible to speak thus of the relation of the Gospel to other religions? To take only one example: Aurobindo claims it as one of the glories of Hinduism that it has the 'courage' (which Christianity lacks) to worship the evil principle of the universe – represented by Durgha – as well as the good; can the Gospel be said in any sense to fulfil something which is incomplete in this faith? Is there not rather a choice between two mutually incompatible beliefs?

2. In what sense can the 'nobler' elements in the non-Christian religions be regarded as stepping-stones to Christian faith? Is it not the case that it is precisely those who represent the noblest elements in the non-Christian religions who are often most bitterly hostile

to the preaching of the Gospel? Is there not a classic example of this in the fact that the Pharisees, who certainly represented the ethically highest element in the Judaism of the time of Jesus, were those who took the lead in destroying him?

3. In what specific ways can one state that the Holy Spirit is active in the non-Christian religions? Would it be possible to achieve any substantial measure of agreement about a list of such evidences?

One of the most characteristic and influential examples of the kind of thinking which inspired the Edinburgh findings was the book by J. N. Farquhar entitled *The Crown of Hinduism*. This book, which consisted mainly in deeply sympathetic and scholarly studies of various aspects of Hinduism, was written to show that 'Christ provides the fulfilment of each of the highest aspirations and aims of Hinduism'. It was outspoken in its condemnation of evils entrenched in the Hindu system of life, but argued that 'every true motive which in Hinduism has found expression in unclean, debasing or unworthy practices, finds in (Christ) fullest exercise in work for the downtrodden the ignorant, the sick and the sinful. In Him is focused every ray of light that shines in Hinduism.'[1]

This book was warmly praised by A. G. Hogg when it appeared, but Hogg's own writing was one of the powerful factors which eventually undermined the influence of this 'fulfilment' concept.[2] In a book written much later, but summing up the teaching which he had been giving for many years, Hogg wrote: 'I do not see eye to eye with those who have looked for a sympathe-

tic line of missionary approach in the conception that
Christianity is the *finding* of that for which Hinduism
has been only a *seeking*. Hindu faith has known of a
finding as well as a seeking. Moreover, if there is within
Christianity a finding which Hindu faith has not experienced, has this not been, in part, because what has
been sought for is *not* the same? As Rudolf Otto has
said, "the religion of India turns upon an altogether
different axis from the religion of the Bible, so that the
two cannot be regarded as preparation and fulfilment".'
Hogg, whose knowledge of Hinduism was deep and
sympathetic, was able to show that the questions
which Hinduism has asked are not the same as those to
which the Gospel is the answer. There is, says Hogg, a
decisive parting of the ways between Hinduism and
Christianity. Jesus makes a demand for absolute surrender which cannot be compromised by another
claim. But it is impossible to define the relation between
Hinduism and Christianity in terms of the incomplete
and the complete. The one is not the 'crown' of the other.

I pass now to the second of the great series of World
Missionary Conferences, that of Jerusalem 1928. At
Edinburgh there had been some attention to the growth
throughout the world of a positivist spirit having its
origins in the West. There was a suggestion that the
world needed the contribution of Indian idealism to
counteract this growth. But this problem was only on
the periphery of the discussion.

At Jerusalem it was in the centre. At the risk of over-
simplification one may say that the dominating fact at

the 1928 meeting was the rise of secularism, and the central question was the quest for the spiritual values of the non-Christian religions including, for the purpose of this discussion, the religion of secularism. There was some tendency to regard the great religions as allies in the battle against secularism, but this was not the final position of the conference. Secularism was regarded as one among the religions of mankind with which the Christian mission must deal. The final position of the conference is well illustrated by the following extract from its 'message':

To non-Christians also we make our call. We rejoice to think that just because in Jesus Christ the light that lighteneth every man shone forth in its full splendour, we find rays of that same light where he is unknown or even is rejected. We welcome every noble quality in non-Christian persons or systems as further proof that the Father, who sent His Son into the world, has nowhere left Himself without witness.

Thus, merely to give illustration, and making no attempt to estimate the spiritual value of other religions to their adherents, we recognize as part of the one Truth that sense of the Majesty of God and the consequent reverence in worship, which are conspicuous in Islam; the deep sympathy for the world's sorrow and unselfish search for the way of escape, which are at the heart of Buddhism; the desire for contact with ultimate reality conceived as spiritual, which is prominent in Hinduism; the belief in a moral order of the universe and consequent insistence on moral conduct, which are inculcated by Confucianism; the disinterested pursuit of truth and of human welfare which are often found in those who stand for secular civilization but do not accept Christ as their Lord and Saviour.

If the central quest of the conference was for the values of the non-Christian systems, the basic, unanswered theological question was: What is the value of the religious values of the non-Christian religions? In that form the question was put to the conference by a Dutch missionary from the East Indies whose name was to dominate the discussion at a later stage – Hendrik Kraemer. Jerusalem did not really get to grips with that question, and Kraemer was to have an opportunity ten years later to press for an answer. Meanwhile it will be helpful to describe three types of comment, represented at Jerusalem, on the central question of the values of the non-Christian religions.

1. The first is that of the continental theologians, who were concerned by the theological tendencies of the preparatory documents and met as a group in Cairo to formulate their own statement to the meeting. The essential points of this statement may be summarized as follows:

(*a*) The existence of spiritual values in the non-Christian religions is fully acknowledged;

(*b*) However, it is not our business, and we are not authorized, to establish comparisons and contrasts between these values and Christianity;

(*c*) Our business is to announce the Gospel of redemption through Jesus Christ, and to accept this Gospel means a radical break with even the best of the values of the non-Christian religions and a total conversion to Christ.

2. The second comment, representative of the Anglo-Saxon approach to the discussion, is taken from a paper of Archbishop William Temple written after the conference was over. Referring to the anxieties expressed by the continental theologians and others about the

quest for the values of the non-Christian religions, Archbishop Temple wrote:

In some quarters there was a fear that the Council would turn out to be committed, by merely embarking on this enquiry, to some sort of vicious syncretism or to the denial by implication of the uniqueness of the Gospel. Nor can it be denied that there was inevitable risk in the method adopted. But here, as so often, the avoidance of risk merely means the deliberate choice and acceptance of one particular disaster. For how are we to proceed from the assertion of the uniqueness of Christ to its demonstration, unless there is instituted a comparison between the Gospel and other religions at their best?

3. A third comment came from Professor John Macmurray of Edinburgh. I select this because, although it was an individual comment, it points forward in a remarkable way to the later stages of the debate. Macmurray's comment on the discussion may be summarized as follows:

(*a*) There are certainly points in common between Christianity and the other religions; but these are precisely the points which are not specifically Christian but merely religious – and Christianity is not merely a religion.

(*b*) The religions are doomed to disappear in any case with the rise of a scientific, secular way of thinking; to spend time seeking out the values of the non-Christian religions is an archaeological pursuit which is not the business of Christian missions.

(*c*) Unless Christianity is essentially and radically different from the other religions, unless there is a sense in which it is right and they are wrong, there is little justification for the enterprise of Christian missions.

As one surveys the Jerusalem debate from the angle of a later stage in the discussion, the following comments may be in order:

(*a*) The question posed by Kraemer was never really answered. It is indeed doubtful whether the use of the term 'values' to describe the elements in the non-Christian religions which Christians found it possible to approve was a helpful use of language. It certainly did not serve to bring out into the open the real issue which divided the conference – and which still divides Christians.

(*b*) Temple's reply to the continentals was logically devastating. Yet it belongs to a different world from the world in which men face the decision about conversion. Do we really have a vantage point from which we can cooly 'institute a comparison between the Gospel and other religions at their best', without in fact bringing into the process judgments which we have already derived from Christ? Is not the appearance of reasonableness and impartiality deceptive? Is not the language of the continental memorandum nearer to the language of the Bible and to the reality of Christian experience?

(*c*) Macmurray's comment was prophetic of much that has happened since 1928. But it may be said with some confidence that his announcement of the end of religion was premature then – and is premature even now. In spite of all that has been written from within the cultural situation of Western Europe, I think it would be unwise to conclude that the end of religion is a foregone conclusion. Nevertheless the comment of

Macmurray has this great value – that it brings forward sharply the question whether the question of the finality of Christ is really a question about the relation of Christianity, or of the Gospel, to other religions or whether it is a question about the place of Christ in secular history. To that question we shall return. Meanwhile, for the time, Macmurray's voice was not heeded.

The ten years following the Jerusalem Conference were the days of 'the larger evangelism' and of 'The Laymen's Enquiry'. The concern expressed by the continentals at Jerusalem was largely muted, as far as the Anglo-Saxon missionary enterprise was concerned. The voice of Karl Barth had not yet begun seriously to influence Anglo-Saxon missionary thinking. The publication of the Laymen's report provoked a sharp debate and made it a matter of urgency to face again the question of the authority of the Gospel in relation to the non-Christian religions. The man who had asked the crucial question at Jerusalem was invited to write the preparatory volume for the World Missionary Conference of 1938. The resulting work, entitled *The Christian Message in a Non-Christian World*, was to dominate not only the Tambaram Conference but also the ensuing debate for a quarter of a century.[3]

At the risk of shocking over-simplification, the thesis of this epoch-making book may be summarized in the following points:

1. The world of the religions is taken with immense seriousness and studied with profound and scholarly

B

understanding; not for nothing was the author known as 'Sheikh Kraemer'.

2. A sharp distinction is drawn between Christianity and the revelation of God in Jesus Christ. The former belongs to the world of the religions; it can claim no absoluteness or finality.

3. The Christian revelation, as the record of God's self-disclosure in Jesus Christ, is absolutely *sui generis*.

4. A sharp distinction is made between God's act of revelation and religious experience – whether Christian or non-Christian.

The distinction made between Christianity and the Gospel is an important clarification of what was less precisely indicated in the speech of Speer at Edinburgh 1910. It is a very important distinction for the whole debate, but leaves us with some difficult questions about the relation of Christianity to the Gospel. If they can be distinguished, they surely cannot be separated. The distinction made in paragraph 4 above raises still more serious difficulties, and these were to be the subject of much discussion at the Tambaram Conference. It is questionable how far the dichotomy between revelation and religious experience can be pressed, for

(*a*) If God's revelatory act has not been in some measure understood and accepted, there has been no revelation; but if it has been understood and accepted, there has been a religious experience.

(*b*) If there has been a religious experience, for instance of a non-Christian, and if we recognize in this experience (as Kraemer certainly does) sublime elements, can we say that there has been no self-disclosure from the side of God?

(*c*) If we have to admit that there has been a self-disclosure from the side of God, what becomes of the *sui generis* character of the revelation in Christ?

At this point in the discussion we have to listen again to a voice that was extremely important in the preparations for Edinburgh 1910, that of A. G. Hogg of Madras. In the debates at Tambaram centring upon Kraemer's theses, it was Hogg who brought the most searching criticism to bear upon Kraemer's main position. The main points made by Hogg may be summarized as follows:

(*a*) A distinction must be drawn between the non-Christian religions and non-Christian faith. This is analagous to the distinction which Kraemer draws between Christianity and the Gospel. By the 'non-Christian religions' we describe the whole range of religious phenomena as they have appeared in history, with all their mixture of good and bad; by 'non-Christian faith' we describe that central religious experience in which – as Hogg believes – there is a real communion between the believer and God.

(*b*) This non-Christian faith is the result of a real divine self-disclosure. It is not something merely self-generated within the believer. We are bound to recognize in certain forms of non-Christian religious experience a genuine communion between the soul of the believer and God himself.

(*c*) What is disclosed in such religious experience is God himself, not 'bits of religious truth'. God's revelation is revelation of himself, not of more or less adequate propositions about religious truth.

It seems to me that Hogg's argument at this point requires a plain answer. I think that, to the question: Is there a genuine self-disclosure of God in non-Christian religious experience?, one must answer with a plain affirmative. If there is no continuity between non-Christian experience of God and that experience of God which is given through Jesus Christ, then we would have to say that all the Bible translators during these past two hundred and fifty years have been wrong. Wherever the Bible has been translated into one of the languages of the non-western world, the translators have had to make a decision about what word to use for 'God'. Every one of these languages has words – usually many words – among which the translators had to choose. All of them plainly are words which derive their content from non-Christian religious experience. If there is no continuity between this experience and the experience of God to which the Bible bears witness, obviously the translators were wrong in using *any* of these words. They should have invented a word, or transliterated a Hebrew or Greek word. In fact they have nowhere done so, and I do not believe there is anyone who thinks that they should.

Kraemer's considered reply to Hogg on this point is found in his book *Religion and the Christian Faith:*

We have quoted Hogg so extensively because his formulations are of rare religious sensitivity, such as has seldom occured in the age-old discussions on our subject. Hogg is quite alive to the bewildering complexity of the problem. This appears from his statement about India:

'In India, for example, what of divine truth and reality has, owing to the initiative of the self-revealing God, succeeded in shining through to Man is all inevitably stained by the medium of monistic tendency through which it has to break.'

This correct observation of Hogg's is, strange to say, in spite of his serious, thought-provoking questions, and in spite of the partial truth of his answers, an indication of the weakness in this noble and reverent attempt to deal with the problem. Most of the questions he puts come from a too individualistic and purely psychological angle. This has its place, but also its distinct limits, because in this psychological dimension one cannot get further than comparing God-experience with God-experience. The questions Hogg puts on the basis of this are valuable and worthwhile questions, but in the last resort they do not decide the questions of truth.

The observation we have just quoted, again, is right, but it does not dig deep enough. He does not ask what to say in the light of Christ – which is always judgment and mercy in one – about this monistic tendency, which is not a regrettable side-issue but the pride, the most precious possession and most valued achievement (so they feel it) of India. He does not raise the question of how to explain that the Jewish people, prepared as no other people to understand what is meant by the Messiah, the Kingdom of God, the suffering Servant, etc., yet did not recognize God in Him, and rejected God's self-disclosure in Christ with as great a determination as Indians, who are (according to Hogg) unable to understand, by their training in Indian thinking, the biblical account of God's eternal activity of redemption. In the light of such questions the mystery of iniquity, precisely in the 'highest' expressions of the human mind, looms up.[4]

Kraemer makes a valid point when he asks why Hogg has not considered the question of the Pharisees at this point in his argument. How is it that the representatives of the highest, noblest, most ethically advanced religion of the world were those who rejected God's revelation in Jesus? It is indeed true that the mystery of iniquity here looms up. Yet Kraemer presumably would not deny that there was a real revelation of God in the religion which these Pharisees represented. I think that Kraemer does not squarely face the question put by Hogg: Is there a real communion between God and the believer in non-Christian religious experience? I think that this question must be answered with a plain affirmative.

But, if one gives this affirmative answer, there is a further question to be put to Hogg. What is the relation of this 'non-Christian faith' to faith in God through Jesus Christ?

Hogg's answer to this question is that, while Christ is the only permanent and adequate way to the Father, and while – once a man has understood through Christ the depth of the abyss that separates sinful man from holy God – he will see that there is no other way than Christ, nevertheless for those who do not know Christ a way is given albeit a narrow and unreliable way. Hogg puts what he has to say in the form of a parable:

A sleep-walker may safely cross a chasm by the narrowest of shaking planks. He is too absorbed in his dream to realize the full threat of the gulf beneath. But let him wake and he will fall. Now in soul and conscience men are prone to be as inappreciative as the sleep-walker of the abysses they think to pass. And so it may befall that, by narrowest and crookedest of doctrinal bridges, they win across the gulf of doubt to that trustful and obedient faith which the Father loves to reward. But when once Christ has stirred them to wakeful perception of the engulfing depths that divide the guilty conscience from trust in God's liberty and readiness to forgive, then by no other bridge than His Cross can they win again to 'joy and peace in believing'. Where Christ has not yet been spiritually apprehended, there may be other ways than He to the trust in God which enables our Heavenly Father to bestow on a man some measure of communion with Himself. But when Christ succeeds in unveiling for any man the judgment of God on sin, in this very act He cannot help making Himself, for that man, the one and only way. Christ is the only way to God that can remain permanently a throughfare.[5]

It is difficult to feel that this is an adequate answer to the question of the relation between non-Christian experience of God and faith in God through Jesus Christ. At this point Kraemer's question to Hogg is extremely pertinent. Kraemer asks why Hogg does not raise here the question of the Jews. Why is it that those who were most fully prepared for the coming of Christ, those to whom God's self-disclosure came most completely, those who were most near to God, were precisely the ones who rejected the revelation and sought to destroy the Redeemer? It is at this point, as Kraemer rightly says, that the real depths of our problem are opened up. Whatever may be the relation between non-Christian and Christian experience of God, it cannot be described in terms of continuity alone. There certainly is continuity; but somewhere in the argument we have to find place for the tragic fact that it is precisely those who are nearest to God who may also be those who most bitterly reject God's revelation of himself in Jesus. This is not only a matter of the Jews; essentially the same thing is often seen in the contact of the Gospel with the so-called higher religions.

As against Kraemer, Hogg insisted that what is unique in Christianity is not that there is a divine self-disclosure, for God's self-disclosure to believing men is not confined to those who know and accept Jesus.

What is unique, according to Hogg, is the content of
the revelation in Jesus. That content is such as to authen-
ticate itself to our consciences as the revelation of God.
We do not say, says Hogg, that the Gospel is unique
because it is the unique self-disclosure of God; we acknowledge it as the unique self-disclosure of God because
of what we recognize as its content.

This distinction made by Hogg between the uniqueness of the 'happenedness' of revelation and the uniqueness of the content of revelation is one to which we
shall return in the next chapter. If what God reveals
is timeless truth, or if it is simply 'himself' apart from
his purpose and his promise, then this distinction
could be maintained. But if it is true that the content of
revelation is in the form of promise and fulfilment and
its context is the total purpose of God for the world,
then this distinction cannot be maintained.

The questions raised by Kraemer were to dominate
the whole discussion for the twenty-five years following
the Tambaram Conference. Unfortunately the effect
of Kraemer's powerful argument was to break off the
dialogue between Christians and non-Christians which
had begun during the earlier period. That this was not
the intention of Kraemer will be obvious to anyone
who takes the trouble to study his writings. But his
tremendous assertion of the discontinuity between the
revelation of God in Jesus Christ and all human religion seemed to many to have destroyed the area of
meeting which had been opened up by men like Farquhar. Eleven years after Tambaram, at the first con-
fernce of Asian Churches at Bangkok, Dr Visser

t'Hooft sharply challenged the Asian theologians to a more adventurous attempt to penetrate the world of non-Christian religious thought and to take up the dialogue afresh. There were many who were eager to to this, and the ensuing two decades have seen a growing effort on the part of Christians in Asia to engage in serious dialogue with men of other faiths. However, the circumstances in which the debate is conducted are different from those of the period before Tambaram, and the terms of the debate have correspondingly changed.

Before we turn to discuss this question in the next chapter, a brief reference should be made to a widely read book in which the thesis that Christ is the fulfilment of Hinduism has been persuasively argued. I refer to *The Unknown Christ of Hinduism* by Raymond Panikkar.[6] The main part of this book consists of a brilliant exposition of a *sloga* of the *Brahma Sutra*, but this is preceded by a chapter in which Panikkar lays down his fundamental theses. These may be briefly summarized as follows:

1. Christ is the universal redeemer; no one is saved unless it be by him.

2. It follows from the revealed nature of God that he provides for every man the necessary means of salvation.

3. Religion is the way by which men are saved and brought into union with God.

4. Before historical Christianity appeared in India, Hinduism was the means of salvation provided for the people of India.

5. 'The good and bona fide Hindu is saved by Christ and not by Hinduism, but it is through the sacraments of Hinduism, through the message of morality and the good life, through the mysterion that comes down to him through Hinduism, that Christ saves the Hindu normally' (p. 54).

6. 'Hinduism is the starting-point of a religion that culminates in Christianity' (p. 58).

I hope that I have not misrepresented Panikkar's thought by setting out this brief summary. When one looks at it as a whole certain weaknesses are at once apparent.

1. One is inclined to apply to it the famous word of Anselm: *nondum considerasti quanti ponderis sit peccatum*. 'The Son of Man *must* suffer,' said Jesus; if general salvation is a logical deduction from the character of God, why the terrible necessity of the Cross? I do not want to defend un-Christian conceptions of the character of God which often lie behind traditional doctrines about the fate of the non-Christian world. But the Gospel story, centred in the story of the Cross, opens our eyes to the terrible reality of man's estrangement from God in a way which, it would seem, must forever exclude any easy deduction of the salvation of all men of good will from the revealed character of God.

2. It is surely important that, according to this scheme, it is the *good* Hindu who will be saved. By what standard is goodness measured, and how does this relate to the Gospel emphasis upon the fact that Jesus came not for the righteous but for the sinners?

3. It is assumed that religion is the sphere of salva-

tion. Why is this? If the Bible is our guide, we cannot exclude the possibility that precisely religion may be the sphere of damnation – the place where man is farthest from the living God. Surely we must insist that the 'light that lightens every man' shines not only, perhaps not even chiefly, in man's religion; rather we may see it shining in the ordinary fidelities of home, business and national life. The answer which Jesus gave to the question, 'What must I do to be saved?', was the story of the Good Samaritan, in which the two religious figures are plainly on their way to perdition, while the non-religious person is in the way of salvation.

4. In this scheme, Christianity is the culmination of a religion whose starting-point is Hinduism. This is the position of Farquhar again. The line of thinking which had been abandoned in Protestant missionary thinking nearly half a century ago, has come back in Roman Catholic thought. Something similar has become very widely accepted through the teaching given in the Papal Encyclical *Suam Ecclesiam*. The picture given in this document is that of the religions as concentric circles grouped around a centre which is occupied by the Roman Catholic Church. Around this centre is a circle composed of other Christians. Beyond this lie other theists, adherents of pagan religions, and finally, at the outer periphery, those who profess no religion at all. This very simple picture has become, for many people, the model by which they understand the relation between the religions.

It must be said very plainly that this model will not

do. The other religions are not to be understood and measured by their proximity to or remoteness from Christianity. They are not beginnings which are completed in the Gospel. They face in different directions, ask fundamentally different questions and look for other kinds of fulfilment than that which is given in the Gospel. They turn, as Otto said, on different axes. To fit them into this model is to lose any possibility of truly understanding them. Moreover what do the concepts of 'near' and 'far' mean in relation to the crucified and risen Jesus? Is the devout Pharisee nearer or farther than the semi-pagan prostitute? Is the passionate Marxist nearer or farther than the Hindu mystic? Is a man nearer to Christ because he is religious? Is the Gospel the culmination of religion or is it the end of religion?

The sharp questions raised by John Macmurray at the Jerusalem Conference have moved into the centre of the debate. The question of the 'value of the religious values of the non-Christian religions' is no longer the central question. The universal process of secularization has forced the debate into other channels. This has been especially apparent in Asia, where the demand to create modern welfare states in the shortest possible time in place of the old colonial dependencies has stimulated men of all religions to turn their attention much more resolutely to the business of this world. The non-Christian religious traditions are being searched anew to find the resources for the demands of a revolutionary time. And Christians have been impressed by the fact that many of the changes for which missions had laboured in the past are now being carried through with far greater success by secular agencies. There is a strong feeling among Asian Christians that God is at work in this revolutionary process. Consequently the question of the finality of Jesus Christ is posed not so much with respect to his relation to the religious values of the non-Christian religions, as with respect to his meaning for the secular history of mankind.

The discussion of the place of Christianity among the religions is certainly not ended. Religion remains, and will remain, an enormously powerful factor in the lives of men and societies. Whatever may be the relation of the Gospel to religion, the interreligious discussion can never be irrelevant to the understanding of the Gospel. But it is necessary if we are to deal faithfully with our main theme, to ask also the question about the place of the Gospel in the secular history of mankind. To that question we now turn.

NOTES

1. J. N. Farquhar, *The Crown of Hinduism* (London 1913), pp. 457–8.

2. For a detailed account of Hogg's criticism of Farquhar's position see: Eric J. Sharpe, *Not to Destroy but to Fulfil* (Uppsala 1965), pp. 288–92.

3. H. Kraemer, *The Christian Message in a Non-Christian World* (London 1938).

4. H. Kraemer, *Religion and the Christian Faith* (London 1956), pp. 226 f.

5. *The Authority of the Faith* (Tambaram Series, Vol. 1) (1939), pp. 123 f.

6. R. Panikkar, *The Unknown Christ of Hinduism* (London 1965).

III

The Gospel as a Secular Announcement

It is obvious that Christianity shares many of the characteristics of other great world religions. If the word 'religion' covers such things as the practice of individual and corporate worship, prayer, the reading and treasuring of sacred scriptures, then it requires no argument to prove that Christianity is a religion.

But it is also clear that Christianity has much in common with movements which are not normally included under the word 'religion'. It could be convincingly argued, for example, that Christianity has much more in common with Marxism than with Buddhism. There is much evidence to show that modern secularism has its roots in the Bible.

Moreover, as a matter of missionary experience, it may be questioned whether the 'point of contact' between the Gospel and the non-Christian man's experience is normally found in the field of his religious experience. The point at which the Gospel 'comes home' to an ordinary man is very often in relation to some experience of his secular life which has no obvious reference to his religious beliefs and practices. I am thinking of the things that are learned in the home, the human experiences of love and estrangement, of obedience and disobedience, of loyalty and disloyalty, experiences of calamity and deliverance, of bereavement and comfort, of guilt and forgiveness. It is normally in relation to such experiences that the Gospel becomes meaningful to men and women, rather than in relation to some element of their specifically religious belief.

In fact must we not say that Jesus himself found his 'point of contact' with his hearer in the secular rather than in the religious field? His characteristic form of teaching was the parable, and the parables are above all stories of ordinary human secular experience. The new thing which Jesus announced, the kingdom of God as present reality, was to be grasped through a deeper understanding of ordinary human experience. It was, in general, the ordinary non-religious people who understood and followed, while the religious leaders were repelled.

We conclude that, while Christianity is certainly one of the religions, it cannot be fully understood *merely* as one of the religions – even if it be the supreme and culminating one. If we go back to the original records and search there for the meaning of the word 'finality' in relation to Jesus, we will see it in a different way from that which has been our point of view in the preceding chapter. If we meditate upon the Gospels with the word 'finality' in our minds, the passages which will come to mind will be such as the following:

The call addressed to men 'Follow me', with its im-

plied demand for total surrender, and the promise
of life attached to it;

The parable of the wicked husbandmen, in which
Jesus is clearly saying that his coming is God's
final call for repentance;

The opening announcement: 'The time is fulfilled
and the Kingdom of God has drawn near';

The final commission: 'All authority in heaven and
on earth is given to me; go therefore and make disciples . . . and lo I am with you to the end of the
world'.

The Gospel in its original form is the announcement of
an event which is decisive for all men and for the whole
of their life. It is an event which is described in universal, cosmic terms. The announcement implies that in
this event all God's purpose·for the world is being
brought to its fulfilment. We are not dealing here with
a religious message which brings to completion and
perfection the religious teaching of all the ages; we are
dealing with an announcement which concerns the end
of the world. The true meaning of the word 'finality' in
relation to Jesus will be found by penetrating into
the meaning of this announcement.

1. How shall we describe it? Is it a religious or a
secular announcement? It is not the teaching of a new
way of personal salvation after the manner of the
Buddha. Nor is it the announcement of a theocratic
kingdom in the manner of Islam. How are we to describe
it? It is the announcement of an event which concerns
the whole human situation and not merely one aspect

of it – the religious aspect, for example. It is the an-
noucement of the reign of God present and active. It
sends Jesus and his disciples out on a mission which
includes healing the sick and feeding the hungry as well
as preaching the good news and teaching the way of
life. But it does not lead to the creation of a theocratic
welfare state in Israel; it leads to rejection, crucifixion
and death. And yet death is not the end; beyond death
is resurrection and the coming of the new era of the
Spirit – promise and guarantee of a new creation, of
new heavens and a new earth, of the new Jerusalem.

This announcement, then, is something unique. It
is neither simply the announcement of a new religious
doctrine, nor the launching of a new secular programme.
It is not an answer offered to the 'questionableness of
human existence', if by that is meant the existence of
the individual human person. It is rather addressed
to the questionableness of all things considered in
their totality. It is the announcement of the decisive
encounter of God with men – not just with men as
individual 'souls' detachable from their place in human
history, but with mankind as a whole, with human history as a whole, indeed with the whole creation. It
concerns the consummation of all things. Its character
as 'final' lies in this fact.

2. The announcement occurred at a particular point
in history. It cannot be detached and looked at as a
piece of timeless wisdom about the human situation
or about the nature of God. 'Under Pontius Pilate' is
part of its substance. This placing of the announcement as an event in secular history is part of its essen-

tial character. At this point we have to return to the debate between Hogg and Kraemer regarding 'occurrence' and 'content'. Hogg summarized the point at issue as follows: 'Kraemer regards the Gospel as unique because of the uniqueness of the occurrence of revelation; I regard it as unique because of the contents of the revelation.' To this it must be replied that the dilemma is a false one because occurrence is part of the content. The revelation is not the disclosure of eternal truths about the nature of God or the duty of man, which could then be compared – in respect of content – with other alleged revelations. The revelation is the launching of an action which looks to the consummation of all things; its relation to ordinary secular history is of its essence.

It is characteristic of Hindu thought that it regards the question of historicity as unimportant. I have never forgotten the astonishment with which a devout and learned teacher of the Ramakrishnan Mission regarded me when he discovered that I was prepared to rest my whole faith as a Christian upon the substantial historical truth of the record concerning Jesus in the New Testament. To him it seemed axiomatic that such vital matters of religious truth could not be allowed to depend upon the accidents of history. If the truths which Jesus exemplified and taught are true, then they are true always and everywhere, whether a person called Jesus ever lived or not. In sharp contrast to this, I remember also a visit to a great churchman and missionary whom I visited in his extreme old age, and found surrounded by books of the latest radical New

Testament scholarship. When I commented on this he replied: 'Everything depends on what really happened; we must know the results of the latest research.'

A position which is not in practice very different from that of the Hindu *advaitin* is reached by some existentialist interpreters of the New Testament with the help of the distinction which the German language allows between the '*historich*' and the '*geschichtlich*'. The former refers to that which can be established by the work of scientific historical research; the latter to that which vitally and 'existentially' concerns me today. The effect of making this distinction frequently seems to be that there is a complete dichotomy created between a dead past of 'objective facts' which have no meaning for the present, and a living present which may be illuminated for me by the similar experiences of the past, but which stands by itself whatever may or may not have happened in the past. This means that time, in the sense of successiveness, ceases to be significant. The only thing which is real is the present, and the 'finality' of the Gospel message can only mean that it is ultimate for me personally at this moment, not that it gives assurance about what will be at the end of the time series.

In contrast to both of these related positions it seems clear that the writers of the New Testament attached immense importance both to showing that the things recorded really happened, and also to placing them exactly in the continuum of secular history. The constant citation of 'witnesses', the careful statements about place and time, the dating of the main events in terms of secular history, and the words with which several of the books of the New Testament open, all testify to the fact that these writers were describing events which they believed to have happened in the same sense in which they believed that there had been a census when Quirinius was Governor of Syria, In keeping with this realistic attitude to history, they believed that the events which they recorded concerned not just the personal situation of the individual believer, but the end of human and cosmic history as a whole – an end which was still in the future.

It is thus impossible to say, with Hogg, that the uniqueness of the Gospel lies in its content and not in the occurrence of the revelation. Event and content cannot thus be separated. 'Happenedness' is of the essence of the content of the announcement. There is all the difference between a statement about the nature of God, and a report that God has, at a certain time and place, acted in a certain way. In the latter case, the occurrence is the essence of the message. The care which is taken in the New Testament to place the events recorded in the continuum of secular history is in striking contrast to the indifference which is generally shown with regard to the historicity of the events which Hindu piety loves to remember in connection with the character of the gods. There is no serious attempt to relate them to events in secular history, nor is it felt that there would be any advantage to be gained from trying to do so – even if it could be done. Their value is that they illustrate truths about God which would remain true even if these particular events had not happened.

At this point in the argument three comments may be in order.

(*a*) The question of the nature of historic 'facts' is an exceedingly complicated one, on which debate continues. But one thing is surely clear. We can no longer accept a positivist conception of history which supposes that 'facts' are the given data which can and should be isolated and identified apart from any judgment of the historian about their meaning. The raw material of the historian is available to him only in the form of reports which necessarily imply some interpretation. 'In the science of history, the facts are not the first datum, but the last product of a process of abstraction that moves from the traditional interpretations to what is today generally and unquestioningly taken to be "objectivity".'[1] The important word in that sentence is obviously the word 'today'. It is for this reason that history has to be constantly rewritten, and that history has been defined as a continuous conversation between the present and the past (E. H. Carr). The distinction between '*Historie*' and '*Geschichte*' is therefore liable to obscure more than it illuminates. There is no history at all apart from some kind of interpretation of the meaning of past events for the present (or rather, as we shall see later, for what the present believes about the future). There seems to be no adequate ground for saying that the facts which are the subject of the Gospel announcement are outside the realm of historical research. They are part of secular history, the only history that we know. The point about them is that they are taken, in the Gospel announcement, as pointers to the meaning of history as a whole.

(*b*) It belongs to the necessary implications of the Gospel that we abandon the dichotomy between a purely personal, inward and spiritual world – the world of our own experiences and decisions – and the outward world of historical events. This dichotomy is familiar to us today in two forms – in the form of the Hindu distinction between the real world of the self and the realm of Maya; and in the form provided by the modern Western existentialist for whom the only meaning of events is the meaning which the individual gives to them. In either form it is a false dichotomy – seen in the light of the Gospel. We have here, in our own times, a situation parallel to the one which the Church faced when it moved out into the world of popular Hellenistic thought. There it was accepted as axiomatic that there is a dichotomy between the sensible world and the intelligible world – the world accessible to the five senses, and the world known through the processes of reason. Christians, reflecting on their faith, were bound to deny the existence of that dichotomy, and the struggle to achieve and maintain the orthodox statements of the doctrines of the Trinity and of the Person of Christ were part of the struggle of the Church to overcome that dichotomy. The Church in the modern world faces a similar struggle to achieve a right statement of the relation of the self to the worlds of nature and history. Perhaps the immense revolution in human thought about the nature of the human self which is suggested by referring to Darwin, Marx and Freud, has tempted Christians to evade conflict by withdrawing the human self into a private spiritual world separate from the world of nature and history. But the Gospel does not allow us to make that withdrawal. The Gospel refers to an event which is determinative not only for the human soul, but for nature and history in their totalities.

(c) We are therefore bound to accept the fact that to believe the Gospel is to be committed to a total interpretation not merely of the personal spiritual life, but also of world history. All historical thinking necessarily begins from a provisional belief about the story which is to be told. This provisional belief (which must always be kept open for correction) governs the direction in which research is attempted, the selection of material reviewed, and the preliminary judgment passed on the material. Christian faith is a kind of judgment upon the meaning of history as a whole, and it must therefore be ready for an open encounter on the field of secular historiography with the proponents of other interpretations of history. There can be no special reserved enclosure labelled 'religious history' where the Christian can work unmolested by the secular historian. Nor can the Christian, when he turns historian, go out leaving behind him his convictions as a believer, to join in the game on other presuppositions. He must bring with him to the work of historical study his convictions as a Christian, and let their validity and vitality be tested in encounter with others. For Christian faith is itself an interpretation of history.

Having made these three comments, I return to the point from which we started, that the dilemma stated by Hogg is misleading. We cannot be asked to make a choice between the uniqueness of the content of the Gospel, and its uniqueness as an event. The Gospel is the announcement of an event in the secular world, an event in which the whole meaning of human history (and of personal history as part of human history) is opened up. As mere event without content it would be meaningless – a mere receptacle into which one is free to put whatever one happens to believe. But as mere religious teaching – apart from its character as the announcement of an event in secular history – it can make no claim to be unique and final.

3. We must now try to say something about the relation of this event to the rest of human experience and especially human religious experience.

It is an event whose proclamation calls for decision. Perhaps the nearest parallel which could be found in our modern world would be the arrival of a Communist Party worker in a new village. His message will be something like the following:

(*a*) The hour has struck for revolutionary action;
(*b*) Here is a cause which enables you to understand and redirect all your actions;
(*c*) There are comrades already at work for the cause;
(*d*) This is a call to total commitment to the cause and to the Party.

The proclamation of the Gospel has something of the same form:

(*a*) The Reign of God has come near in Jesus;

(*b*) To accept it means to be able to understand and direct all your action – both private and public;

(*c*) There is an apostolic fellowship of those who are already committed and at work;

(*d*) This is the call to you to like commitment.

What does this proclamation and summons mean for the interpretation of human experience, and especially of human religious experience, apart from and before the acceptance of the Gospel?

(i) It does not mean that the reality of religious experience outside of faith in Jesus Christ is denied. At this point, as I have said, it seems to me that Kraemer is insufficiently forth-right. If acceptance of Jesus Christ as the revelation of God means the denial of reality to alleged communion with God apart from faith in Christ, then we have all been wrong in using the non-Christian words for 'God' in our translations of the Bible and in the life and worship of the Church.

(ii) Nevertheless, having said this, it must also be said that acceptance of Jesus Christ as Lord means radical repentance and conversion from all pre-Christian religious experience. The focus of the Gospel is the word of the Cross, and that word is a radical judgment upon all human wisdom and upon the experience on which that wisdom is founded. This refers not only to 'religious' wisdom but equally to man's 'secular' wisdom. The word of the Cross confronts us with the fact that, in the presence of God incarnate in a human life, both man's religious wisdom, embodied in the representatives of Jewish prophetic religion, and man's secular wisdom, embodied in the representative of Roman law, are exposed as radical hostility to the truth of God. This radical judgment upon all human wisdom is foreshadowed in the teaching of Jesus; it is concentrated in a burning focus in the Cross. Here is the basis of that judgment upon human nature which is embodied in the Christian doctrine of original sin. It is in the presence of the Cross that we are compelled to say: There is none righteous, no not one.

This radical judgment is not simply a judgment upon human religion. It is perhaps significant that, in the Gospel record, the first word of penitent acknowledgment of this judgment is spoken out of a purely secular context: it was the Roman centurion, responsible for carrying out the execution, who was the first to confess that this 'criminal' was indeed righteous. But the judgment includes a judgment upon human religion. The religious leaders were those who played the decisive role in bringing about the death of Jesus, and the religon they represented was very high religion – the lineal descendant of the religion of the prophets. But in the presence of Christ even this – nay, especially this – is exposed as hostility to the truth of God. The radical judgment of human religion which is embodied in the Cross is fully worked out in the writings of St Paul. Among many passages which might be quoted, let me refer simply to the autobiographical section in Philippians 3, where, after listing the treasures which were his as a devout Pharisee, Paul goes on to say that in the light of Christ he is compelled to regard all this as refuse and to cast it all away in order that he may gain Christ and be found in him.

The total fact of the Cross, which is the focus of the Gospel, makes it impossible to describe the relationship between faith in Christ and other forms of religious commitment in terms simply of continuity and fulfilment. There is a radical discontinuity.

(iii) And yet it is not a total discontinuity. When St Paul, writing as a Christian believer, looks back upon his own story and upon the story of his race, he sees working in it the living God whom he knows in Christ. It was the same living God who made his covenant with Abraham and who gave to his descendants the law, the liturgy and the promises (Romans 9.4). It was the same living God who had been dealing with him when he was a Pharisee, even though he was himself fighting against God. And even when he preaches to the pagan Athenians he takes as his starting-point their worship of 'an unknown God' and tells them – in effect – that even in their pagan worship it was the living and truce God whom they were seeking. This element of continuity is confirmed in the experience of many who have become converts to Christianity from other religions. Even though this conversion involves a radical discontinuity, yet there is very often the strong conviction afterwards that it was the living and true God who was dealing with them in the days of their pre-Christian wrestlings.

One may sum up the three points which I have tried to make in some such way as the following: the Gospel has a double relationship to man's experience, and to the wisdom founded upon it, apart from the knowledge of God in Jesus Christ. It is a relationship both of continuity and of discontinuity. The Gospel demands and effects a radical break with, and conversion from, the wisdom that is based upon other experience; yet mature reflection by those who have experienced this break suggests that it is the same God who has been dealing with them all along. He has never been without witness even when they did not know him as he has revealed himself in Jesus.

4. When the Gospel event and the Gospel announcement are seen – as we have tried to see them – in the context of the New Testament, it becomes clear that much of the discussion about the relation of Christianity to the other religions is based upon false premises. The form which this discussion usually takes is the form of the question: will the pious Hindu (or Muslim, or Buddhist) be saved? In the light of the previous discussion about the meaning of the Gospel announcement, it will be seen that this question is posed in the wrong form. Two comments seem to be in order.

(i) The meaning of the word 'saved' in the question needs to be examined. As the question is normally put, it refers solely to something which is to happen to the person after death. Behind the question in this form lies a concept of salvation which is as widespread among Christians as it is remote from the New Testament. It is a concept of salvation which restricts the term to something which may or may not happen to the individual soul after death. But in the New Testament this is not the meaning of salvation, or of the final work of Christ. The New Testament picture is dominated by the great corporate and cosmic completion of God's work in Christ, whereby all things will be restored to the unity for which they were created in Christ, and God will be all in all. In that final consummation the whole history of the world, as well as the history of each human soul, will find its true end. To be saved is to participate – in fore-taste now and in fulness at the end – in this final victory of Christ. According to the New Testament, the coming of Christ, his dying and rising and ascension, is the decisive moment in God's plan of salvation, presenting to every man who hears of it the opportunity and the necessity for faith, repentance, conversion and commitment to participation in the work of God in this present age. It is certainly made clear that it is possible to refuse this opportunity and thereby to lose the possibility of salvation – to be lost. But it is not, I believe, implied that the vast multitudes who have never been presented with this Gospel call for conversion and commitment are thereby necessarily excluded from participation in God's on-going and completed work.

(ii) The question: are there few that be saved? is one that Jesus declined to answer. It is a question which seems to fascinate many Christian minds today. There are, on the one hand, those who seem anxious to keep the doors of hell wide open so that there may not be any lack of funds and recruits for missionary work. There are, on the other hand, those who seem to think that God governs the universe on some sort of referendum principle, and that it is intrinsically impossible that the majority might be wrong. It therefore appears to them that, since the unbelievers in all the range of human history are far more than the believers, it follows that God saves on other grounds than faith.

Neither of these positions has any real ground. We have no data to answer the question. When it was put to Jesus his only reply was to advise the questioners to do their best to get in through the narrow door. We have no means of going beyond that answer. We are confronted with the total fact of Christ, crucified and risen. We are given the opportunity to repent, to believe, to be converted, to be committed to the doing of his will in this present world. We are not offered something which might be described as the best among the religions; we are offered something which, if it is true, is the clue to all history – the history of the world, and the history of my own soul.

Before going on to explore more fully what it means to speak of the Gospel as the clue to history, I append two footnotes to the discussion of this chapter.

(i) I draw attention again to the point made at the beginning: everything in this discussion depends upon the starting-point. One could begin a discussion of 'the finality of Christ' by taking the concept of 'religious experience' as the starting-point. This is what Hocking does in his discussion of these issues. One can begin by seeking to discern that which is common to and central in all human religious experience. One can seek to define that as sharply as possible. And one can then go on to ask: what conditions would a historic event have to fulfil in order to be properly described as 'final' for religious experience? Or, on the other hand, one can begin with the historic fact of Christ – his life, death and resurrection – accepted and understood as the decisive and final event for my life and for all creation. One can then explore what that acceptance and understanding means both for religious experience and for the totality of human secular experience. You cannot demonstrate in advance that either of these is the right starting-point; if you could do so, it would not be the starting-point. The starting-point is a decision of faith, and it is validated – if at all – only as the outcome of this process of exploration.

(ii) I referred at the end of the first chapter to the situation in Asia, where the discussion today is largely shaped by the response of all the religions to the process of secularization. The discussion in this chapter has shown, I hope, that this is not merely an accidental happening. It is not by accident that the point of contact between the Gospel and the other religions is seen increasingly to be in the secular field. Nor can the Christian view the process of secularization in Asia as simply an accidental change of climate. If he understands the Gospel rightly, he will be able to see the integral connection between the impact of the biblical conception of God upon Asia and the process of secularization, and to see that the real clue to the meaning of the process of secularization is to be found in the Gospel. Rightly understood, the process of secularization is an extending of the area of freedom wherein man has the opportunity to understand and respond to what God has done for the world in Jesus Christ.

But to say this is already to enter upon the subject of the ensuing chapter. To speak of the finality of Christ must mean to claim that in Christ there is found the clue to history, and therefore to participation in the history of our times. It must be our next business to explore the meaning of that claim.

NOTE

1. Jürgen Moltmann, *Theology of Hope* (London and New York 1967), p. 241.

IV

The Clue to History

Our argument hitherto has been that the question of
the finality of Christ is not simply a question of the
relation of Christianity or of the Gospel to other religions; it is a question of the place of Jesus Christ in
universal history. To speak of the finality of Christ is
to speak of the Gospel as the clue to history. What
does it mean thus to speak?

1. In the first place it means that one takes one's
stand on one side of what Nicol Macnicol calls 'the
great divide among the religions'; one confesses the
faith that history means something. If religion is concerned about that which finally controls and unifies
all experience, then it is clear that in principle there are
two ways which it can go. There are in principle two
ways in which one can seek unity and coherence behind
or beyond all the multiplicity and incoherence which
human experience presents to us. One way is to seek
unity as an existent reality behind the multiplicity of
phenomena; the other is to seek unity as an end yet
to be obtained. The typical picture of the first is the
wheel; of the second, the road.

Although the wheel is a human construct, it is a
c

powerfully evocative symbol of the natural world as man experiences it. The cycle of birth, growth, decay and death through which plants, animals, human beings and institutions all pass suggests the rotating wheel – ever in movement yet ever returning upon itself. The wheel offers a way of escape from this endless and meaningless movement. One can find a way to the centre where all is still, and one can observe the ceaseless movement without being involved in it. There are many spokes connecting the circumference with the centre. The wise man will not quarrel about which spoke should be chosen. Any one will do, provided it leads to the centre. Dispute among the different 'ways' of salvation is pointless; all that matters is that those who follow them should find their way to that timeless, motionless centre where all is peace, and where one can understand all the endless movement and change which makes up human history – understand that it goes nowhere and means nothing.

The other symbol is the road. History is a journey, a pilgrimage. We do not yet see the goal, but we believe in it and seek it. The movement in which we are involved is not meaningless movement; it is movement towards a goal. The goal, the ultimate resting-place, the experience of coherence and harmony, is not to be had save at the end of the road. The perfect goal is not a timeless reality hidden now behind the multiplicity and change which we experience; it is yet to be achieved; it lies at the end of the road.

This, very roughly sketched, is what Macnicol calls 'the great divide'. Many writers on religion do not acknowledge it as such. Too often, it seems, writers on the comparative study of religion assume that the essence of religion lies in the mystical experience and therefore take their stand, without argument, on one side of the divide. Starting from this conviction, they find evidences in all religions of this experience in varying forms and with varying depths – but all recognizable as belonging to the same kind. Obviously different religions have different attitudes to history, but these differences are taken to be variations within one fundamentally homogeneous reality, different dialects of one language. There is no 'great divide'.

Paul Tillich, in his report on his discussion with Buddhists,[1] treats what we have called the great divide as a polarity within a single system. Both Christianity and Buddhism, he says, grow out of 'the experience of the Holy here and now'. In one the mystical predominates, and in the other the ethical. In one holiness is what ought to be (the Kingdom of God), and in the other holiness is what is (Nirvana). This leads to divergent attitudes towards history. But, says Tillich, there is a non-historical mystical element in Christianity, and – on the other hand – 'history itself has driven Buddhism to take history seriously'. On this the following comments would seem to be in order.

(*a*) Manifestly Christianity and Buddhism, as religious systems which have existed through many centuries and have been involved with other cultural and religious forces throughout these centuries, have been influenced by factors other than those which originally gave them birth. Christianity has, from the moment that the Gospel broke into the Hellenistic world, been in contact with, and influenced by pantheistic religion and by the kind of mysticism which flourishes in a pantheistic environment. Nevertheless the basic structure of the Christian Scriptures, creeds and liturgies is such as to make it impossible for this kind of mysticism ever to have the central place. Nothing can displace the concrete historic figure of Jesus Christ from the centre of the Christian religion. And on the other hand the modern development of a unified secular world-society has compelled Buddhism to take history seriously. Nevertheless this development is not just an accidental fact of history; it is intimately related to the world-wide spread of the secularized form of the biblical conception of the Kingdom of God which has its roots in Christendom. From a Christian point of view this development is part of the consequences of the incarnation – the drawing of all men out of a non-historical form of existence into a single global history dominated by issues which have been raised for man by the biblical revelation.

(*b*) We may accept the statement that both religions grow out of 'the experience of the Holy here and now'.[2] But the question is: What is the character of the Holy? or, Who is the Holy One? It is an obscuring of the issues to speak of 'Holiness as what is' and 'Holiness as what ought to be' as though they were the end-readings on a scale across which the needle could swing back and forth without a break. The revelation of God which is concentrated in the Cross of Jesus Christ is the revelation of a holiness which *is* and which is in agony until what ought to be is. That agony is in history, and if history is not taken seriously the revelation is not received. For Christianity the deepest meaning of history lies in the fact that in it God, who *is*, is wrestling with the estranged and rebellious wills of men, until his own perfect love is embodied and reflected in a redeemed and restored creation. That is necessarily involved in taking the total fact of Christ, with its burning centre in the Cross, as the object of faith. *Per contra* I have found in discussion with Hindu friends that, while they will generally seek to interpret Christian experience and doctrine from within the perspective of the Vedanta, they generally acknowledge that at the point of the attitude to history there is a radical difference between what Christians believe and what the Hindu view of life permits. There is, it seems to me, good reason for agreeing with Macnicol that this is 'the great divide' among the religions.

2. To speak of Christ as the clue to history means that history is understood as in some sense a coherent whole. This is not obvious. History appears to be full of incoherence and meaninglessness. Moreover history as normally understood is the history of some part of the human race or of some aspect of human culture. One can understand what is meant by the history of India, or the history of European architecture, or of Arctic exploration. Until very recent times the conditions did not exist for writing a universal history which could include in one work substantial material covering all the continents and all the races of mankind through all the millennia of human existence on the planet.

There was not enough mutual contact between the great races and cultures, and there was not enough knowledge of the past. What was called 'universal history' was – until relatively recent times – history based upon the Bible, written by men who were ignorant of vast tracts of human history, but who took their stand upon the biblical faith concerning the origin and destiny of man. In recent times it has been common to regard this kind of 'universal history' as invalid; it is easy to point to its limitations and to conclude that it is really a very local or provincial essay in history, not different basically from, say, a history of Europe into which the rest of the world comes only as it impinges upon the consciousness of European man.

Since Voltaire there have been many efforts to construct a universal history which would be genuinely universal – free from the limitations and prejudices of the western Christian tradition, history written in an objective, impartial spirit which sees all mankind and all human history as equally worthy of record. But the matter has only to be stated in that way to reveal its intrinsic impossibility. All historical writing involves the selection of the most significant from among the almost infinite mass of records. The selection is necessarily based upon the provisional judgment of the historian, which again depends upon his own understanding of and commitment to the course of events in his own time. Histories which claim to be free from any sectional or provincial prejudice cannot conceal from the critical reader the convictions which led the historian to proceed in the way he did. His convictions may be so much the unexamined convictions of his age and place that his first readers do not notice them, and are convinced by the claim to objectivity and impartiality But readers of another age and place will immediately recognize that his axiomatic convictions are indeed highly questionable.

If all history is to be grasped as a unity, it must be from some standpoint, and, as I have already said, there is no standpoint which is above all particular standpoints. A man can only see things from where he is. How then can there be such a thing as a universal history?

Normally a story can only be well told by a man who sees the point of the story before he begins to tell it. If he does not see the point, his tale will get lost in a mass of irelevant detail. If the detail includes (as it does in the story we are considering) all the available records of the whole life of man in every age and country, the possibility of getting lost is very great. But how does one grasp the point? Normally the point is only clear at the end; we are still in the middle of the story. How, then, can there be a universal history? Only if, by some means, the teller has become convinced about the end of the story while he is still in the midst of it. Such a conviction will necessarily be at the same time a commitment to act in a certain way in the history which is being written today and tomorrow.

To speak of the finality of Christ is to express such a conviction and such a commitment concerning the point of the human story as a whole. A secular historian writing a universal history is – explicitly or implicitly –

expressing such a conviction and commitment. It is a conviction which can be criticized. It is not a point of vantage above all sectional standpoints. It is vulnerable. But without accepting the risks which it involves, there can be no universal history.

In this respect there is no difference in principle between the Christian theologian's way of handling the historical records of his faith and those of a secular historian. Both of them are taking the risks which are involved in making a judgment about the data; they differ about the 'end' which determines the meaning of everything that goes before it. 'The faith which is needed to interpret the Bible is not in principle different from the faith with which any secular historian handles his material.'[3]

Once again, therefore, to speak of the finality of Christ is to speak of him as the clue to our interpretation of history as a whole. It implies that our conviction about Christ, and our commitment to serve him in the present hour, gives us the standpoint from which we can truly understand human history as a whole. It therefore involves us in a discussion not merely with the adherents of other religions but with all men who are seeking to understand the human situation and to discern the kind of commitment which is required for playing a responsible part in the ongoing history of which we are a part.

What, exactly, is it for which we claim finality? It is not 'Christianity'. On that probably all Protestant Christians would agree. We have seen how both at Edinburgh in 1910 and at Tambaram in 1938 – though with differing terminology – the point was clearly made that we claim no sort of finality for the body of beliefs and practices which is included under the heading 'Christianity'. Christianity is a changing and developing corpus of belief, practice, association, cultus, which is all the time assimilating new elements from other religions and other world views, and which needs, therefore, criteria by which it can determine what is true development and what is distorted or cancerous growth. We cannot claim finality for Christianity.

I have said that probably all Protestant Christians would agree about this. It is not clear whether Roman Catholics would do so. In the Encyclical *Suam Ecclesiam*, to which reference has already been made, the Pope, in introducing the picture of the religions as concentric circles says: 'We think the situation can be described as consisting of a series of concentric circles around the central point in which God has placed Us.' This sentence concisely summarizes what the encyclical as a whole teaches, namely that the Roman Catholic Church, with the Pope at its head, is the criterion by which other religious beliefs are understood and evaluated. It seems, as plainly as possible, to teach the finality of the Roman Catholic Church, and it contains warnings against the idea that the concept of reform could be applied 'either to the essential conception of the Church or to its basic structure' (p. 24). Yet, as is well known, other voices in the Roman Catholic Church are speaking of the possibility of reform in a much more fundamental sense.

Be that as it may – and it is a matter of enormous

importance for all Christians – it is safe to say that
Protestants do not claim finality for Christianity in
any of its empirical manifestations; they claim finality
for Christ. But what does that claim mean, when dif-
ferentiated from a claim on behalf of Christianity?
What are the implications of making a radical disjunction between Christ and Christianity or between
the Gospel and Christianity? It is one of the small
ironies of history that the same Tambaram Conference
which witnessed the most resounding statement of the
distinction between the Gospel and Christianity was also
the meeting which insisted upon the centrality of the
Church to the missionary task, which insisted that the
Church is in fact part of the Gospel. It is well known
that the missionary thinking of the years preceding the
Tambaram Conference had given little place to the
Church and had been inclined to speak more of the
Kingdom of God. Tambaram emphatically and deliber-
ately turned the thinking of the Churches in a different
direction, and made the Church the centre of its thinking about the missionary task. The Tambaram discussion is therefore a good starting-point for posing the
question: what exactly is involved in making a disjunction between Christianity and the Gospel?

(*a*) I have already referred to the argument of Hogg
that a distinction analogous to that made by Kraemer
between the Gospel and Christianity must also be made
between Hinduism as a total system of belief and practice, and the faith of a devout Hindu. In reply to this
Kraemer had little difficulty in showing that it was not
a true analogy, for the thing for which he claimed

finality was not the faith of the devout Christian but the Gospel – the message of God's unique and decisive self-revelation in Jesus Christ, Incarnate, Crucified, Risen.

(b) This reply of Kraemer's is, as we have already seen, open to criticism, and we must now develop the criticism further. It is impossible to make a total disjunction of revelation and faith, for if there is no faith by which the revelation is grasped, there is no revelation. Revelation happens when God actually communicates himself to men, and that communication happens only if there is human response. The decisive revelation cannot be described altogether apart from the human response of faith. Moreover at this point we have again to listen to the historian. I have already drawn attention to the fact that historians cannot make a total disjunction between so-called 'facts' and their interpretation. A 'fact of history' is an interpretation of evidence. The 'fact of Christ' (to use the phrase beloved of my old teacher Dr Carnegie Simpson) is the life, death and resurrection of Jesus interpreted by the apostles. Apart from their faith, the very name of Jesus would be unknown to us; there would be no 'fact of Christ' for us to believe in. Like other facts of history, the fact of Christ is available to us now because of the judgment of contemporaries about its significance. The 'fact' cannot be had in isolation from the judgment, even though the judgment is always subject to our critical examination. E. H. Carr's definition of the nature of history could also be applied to the work of Christian theological thinking: it is a continuous conversation between the believer of today and the first believers – the apostles.

(*c*) To claim finality for Christ is to endorse the judgment of the apostles that in this life, death and resurrection God himself was uniquely present and that therefore the meaning and origin and end of all things was disclosed; it is to join with the apostles in making this judgment.

This does not mean that, whereas God is always revealing himself in all times and places, it happened that at this time and place there were those who recognized and responded; that would be to claim uniqueness for the apostles, not for Christ. If this were all we meant by the fact of Christ, then we could not claim finality for this; for we could expect others at other times and places to respond even more adequately. The Christian faith, based upon the apostolic testimony, is that in the whole course of history, which is in some sense a unity, this is the decisive point, the turning-point; and that at this turning-point both the event and the true interpretation of the event were – by God's overruling activity – made possible. It is of the substance of what we mean by 'the fact of Christ' that in God's long and patient wrestling with the human race, this time and place were made ready, this people was prepared, these men were chosen and trained in order that they might be the witnesses and interpreters of this unique and decisive event.

(*d*) I have said that to speak of the finality of Christ is to endorse the apostolic testimony concerning him. But a further point has now to be made. We do not know about this apostolic testimony in the way that an archaeologist learns about a remote and long-buried civilization. We know about it because we have been made part of a continuous tradition, carried by a community in which the writings of these apostles have been continuously treasured, reproduced, studied, expounded, interpreted and applied to changing situations. It is as part of this living, doubtless changing, but also continuing tradition that we speak about the finality of Christ. Without this, the apostolic testimony would not be a significant fact of our own present experience. To claim, for instance, that some event which took place during the history of the Mohenjo Daro civilization or among the Incas of Peru was the decisive turning-point of human history would be meaningless. We are not connected with it in any way which involves our present experience. The claim that the fact of Christ is decisive for all human life is a meaningless claim except as it is interpreted in the life of a community which lives by the tradition of the apostolic testimony. There cannot, therefore, be a total disjunction between the Gospel and 'Christianity'. To claim finality for Christ means *in some sense* to claim a decisive role in history for the Church.

The answer to the obvious question: 'in what sense?' will have to be developed when we come to speak of conversion to Christ and his Church. Here, however, the following point must be made. The original apostolic witness remains permanently at the centre of the life of the Church in order to provide the norm by which all subsequent development is judged and by which aberrations are corrected. There must be development. It is impossible simply to go on repeating the original words. They have – in the first place – to be translated, and all translation changes meaning. They have, then, to be re-interpreted to meet new situations. It is precisely by the vigour and courage with which the work of re-interpretation is done that the claim to finality is made good in the actual course of human history. Only when the Church has the boldness to re-interpret the original testimony in the face of new human situations is it able to make plain and effective the claim to finality. Re-interpretation always carries risks, but to evade risks always means to court disaster. Syncretism is not the only danger against which the Church has to be alert. The New Testament is equally clear in its warnings against the opposite danger – the danger of timidity, of trying to avoid risks by tying up the talent in a napkin to be preserved in useless safety until the Lord's return. In this necessary and dangerous work of re-interpretation the Church has to take its bearings by means of the original witness of the apostles. This acts as a norm of development, a source of reform when life and message have been distorted by being conformed to the whims of a passing age, and a fount of renewal when life has been stifled by too much caution and by a false isolation from the world.

(*e*) The apostolic testimony to Jesus as Lord is a claim for his finality in respect of matters of which the apostles themselves were necessarily ignorant. They knew nothing of Buddhism or Hinduism, yet claimed that

Jesus was the only name given under heaven whereby we must be saved. They knew nothing of the sort of future for the human race which we are glimpsing in the second half of the twentieth century, yet they confessed him as the *alpha* and the *omega*, the beginning and end of all things.

In this respect Christian faith is analogous not only to the judgment of a historian, but also to the generalization of a natural scientist or mathematician. Like the great theorems of science and mathematics, it is a statement which, if true, implies much more than the person who first made it could possibly be aware of. Its truth will be confirmed by discoveries which lie far beyond the horizon of its originator. This has implications which may be stated both negatively and positively.

(i) Negatively it means that faith in Christ does not give the believer a total picture of human history which excuses him from the necessity of making new discoveries. He is not in a position to read off a chart of world history from creation to consummation out of the material given in the Bible. This is a point at which Christians have frequently been mistaken. There is a real sense in which the Bible is a universal history, telling the story of the world from its origin to its end. But its accounts of the beginning and the end are imaginative and parabolic proclamations of its faith that the clue to the whole is to be found at the centre; of its faith that the origin and end not only of human history but of cosmic history (and the Bible requires us to work with this conception) are to be understood in terms of that series of events in which God has decisively acted and thereby revealed his character and his intention.

(ii) Positively one can state the claim in the following way. The community which lives in the fellowship of commitment to Christ as Lord, while not thereby given any detailed map of the course of history, is enabled by faith to participate in the struggles of human history in such a way as not to be in vain. To put the matter in another way: the kind of commitment to action in history which arises from faith in Christ will be found – in all the vast and unforeseeable changes of the human situation, changes which the first apostles could never have imagined – to be fruitful, creative, constructive.

Thus the claim is certainly not that Christianity is final. It is that through participation in the corporate life of the community which – founded upon the apostolic testimony – is committed to Christ as Lord, one is enabled rightly to interpret God's work in human history, and thereby rightly to commit oneself to constructive action in history. It is the claim that, at the end of the story, this will be seen to have been the true, the proper, the relevant commitment.

4. But can we, even on the basis of faith in Christ, really interpret history? There is a mass of depressing evidence which could be cited against any claim to be able to do so. One thinks of all the cranks and fanatics down the ages, and in our own day, who claim to understand exactly what God is doing in contemporary history. One thinks of all the expert students of the Books of Daniel and Revelation who claim to foretell the events of the 1970's. One thinks of the German

Christians in the 1930's confidently interpreting the rise of the Nazi movement as God's cleansing action on behalf of the German people. It is understandable that those who went through the terrible experiences of Nazi rule, and others also, should express some alarm when they hear Christians claim to know what God is doing in the political and cultural and technological revolutions of our time.

One may grant that there is ground for this alarm, and yet one must press the question: how can we possibly *refuse* to try to interpret what God is doing in the secular events of our time? If we were to do so, we should be parting company with the prophets and with Jesus himself. The very heart of the prophetic message was their inspired interpretation of the events of their time – wars, enslavements, liberations, droughts, plagues and famines – in terms of the purpose of the living God. And Jesus himself, it seems, repeatedly told his hearers that they ought to be able to discern the signs of the times just as they knew how to interpret the changes in the sky and the winds. Whatever be the dangers of this enterprise, are we permitted to abandon it?

Moreover, what is the alternative? If I am to commit myself in any way to taking part in the public life of my time, it must be on the basis of some interpretation of what is going on, of what are the issues, of what are the forces at work. If I decline to attempt any interpretation, I must also avoid any commitment and confine myself to keeping my own personal record clean – if that is possible in a world so full of evil. And if I refuse that dereliction of duty and commit myself to action in the public realm, where am I to find the guidelines if not in my faith in Jesus Christ?

A recent discussion in the pages of the *Ecumenical Review* has brought this issue very sharply into focus as it relates to the situation in Asia. Dr H. H. Wolf, drawing on his experience of German theological struggles, seriously questions the language used by Mr M. M. Thomas about discerning the work of God in the renaissance of the Asian religions and the multiple revolution which dominates the Asian scene today. The anxiety of Dr Wolf is understandable; but the reply of Mr Thomas is also justified. At the point of the effort to interpret current history, the Christian cannot simply leave a vacuum.[4] If history is not a meaningless jumble of events, if God is working out a purpose in it, it is necessary to try to interpret – even if only in very modest, tentative and provisional terms – what he is doing. If we are to know where to act, where to throw our weight, where to commit ourselves, we must have some provisional answer to the question: Where is God at work and where is the Devil?

Perhaps our greatest temptation lies at the following point: it is easy, in effect, to translate the faith that God is at work in history into the proposition that where a movement appears to be successful there God must be at work. It is easy to think of examples of what – at least with the benefit of hindsight – looks like this fatal error. The assurance, for instance, with which many western Protestant Christians regarded the spread of western power all over the world, and the consequent expansion of the opportunities for missionary work as a sign of the activity of God, is an example that comes readily to mind. Other similar convictions may be more disputable because they are nearer to our own day. Obviously there is here a very plausible temptation. Moreover no one can deny that the conviction that God is on our side can give an unequalled vigour and vitality to any movement.

Recognizing these dangers, what practical content can we give to the faith that God is working out his purpose in history and that the clue to this purpose is to be found in Jesus Christ? How are we to interpret God's action in history and so learn to commit ourselves to obedient partnership?

In this difficult matter I would suggest the following three-fold statement of the Christian claim:

(*a*) That which is disclosed in Jesus Christ is the very character and will from which all that is proceeds. For the believer who, by the work of God's Spirit, has been brought to stand before the Cross of Christ and to give his Amen to the apostolic testimony about it, this is thenceforth the commitment by which all else is judged. It arises from a total personal experience, which the New Testament calls the new birth, in which a man is brought to abandon all other commitments and to commit himself wholly and without reserve to Jesus Christ in the fellowship of those who share the same commitment.

To one who has made that commitment, the disclosure of God in Jesus Christ is determinative of his interpretation of all the events of history. Wherever he sees men being set free for responsible sonship of God; wherever he sees the growth of mutual responsibility of man for man and of people for people; wherever he sees evidences of the character of Jesus Christ being reflected in the lives of men; there he will conclude that God is at work, and that he is summoned to be God's fellow-worker, even where the Name of Christ is not acknowledged. By contrast, wherever he sees the reverse process at work, men being enslaved, mutual responsibility being denied, and the opposite of the character of Christ being produced in men; there he will recognize the work of the Devil and will know himself summoned to resist.

Jesus Christ is the sole criterion. Here we have to take our stand with the Barmen Declaration. There is no other source of revelation, once we have known Christ.

(b) This disclosure of the character and will of God in the midst of human history is met not by success but by rejection. Jesus is crucified; his Church is persecuted; those who follow him are promised suffering, rejection and death. There is emphatically no equation between faithfulness to God's will and success in history. To follow Christ means to deny self and accept the Cross. Therefore the Christian who commits himself to the kind of action in history just described will not be deflected or defeated when he and the causes which he supports meet rejection. He will accept this as part of his participation in God's struggle with man which is the stuff of history.

(c) But this is not the last word. If it were, Christian discipleship could only be a flight from history. Jesus rises from the dead. The tomb is empty. Jesus is declared to be the Son of God with power. This is a fact of history in the only sense in which we can speak of a fact of history, namely a judgment of the evidence. The Christian believes that this judgment is determinative for the understanding of all history, that it is the point at which the meaning of the whole story is disclosed, and that the whole story must therefore be understood from this point.

While recognizing the very great problems which these assertions raise, I would submit that if, at this point, we fall back into a dichotomy of inward and outward, making the resurrection only an event in the internal spiritual history of the disciples and not an event in the history of Jesus and therefore of the world, then we abandon the possibility of claiming that Jesus is the clue to history.

Because of his resurrection faith, the Christian will expect and will find that defeat is turned into victory; that even in the midst of the appalling triumph of human blindness and wicked-ness, evidences will be continually forthcoming – manifest to eyes of faith – of the victory of God. 'Manifest to eyes of faith.' Like the resurrection itself, these evidences of God's victory in the life of the world will be – not 'facts' which could be demonstrated irresistibly to any person irrespective of his personal judgment – but confirmations of that judgment of faith which recognizes in the resurrection of Jesus the decisive act of God. The claim that Jesus is final is the claim that at the end of the story this judgment will be seen to be the true judgment, the true interpretation of history, and the action arising out of commitment to that judgment to be the ultimately significant action.

I think that we can go a step further. As the Christian looks back over the course of human history, as it is unfolded by the work of scholars, and over the still vaster course of cosmic history as it is deciphered by biologists, palaeontologists and astronomers, and as he seeks to interpret it from the standpoint of the revelation of God in Jesus Christ, he sees signs which confirm the understanding which is given to him in the Bible: a growing mastery of man over nature, a growing interdependence of all men with one another, larger areas of freedom and therefore of responsibility. As he looks to the future, the Christian sees the pattern of Cross and Resurrection as the key to its interpretation: the rejection by man of God's love; the use of the greater and greater freedom and power which God gives to man for more and more disastrous rebellion against God; and yet the infinite power and resourcefulness of God to use men's rebellion as the means to his victory; the pattern of Cross and Resurrection thrown on to the screen of world history in the shape of the New Testament figures of the Antichrist and the Millennium; the ultimate assurance of God's victory in this world and over this world – even though the relation between this 'in' and this 'over' remains hidden from us.

To claim finality for Christ is to claim that this is the true clue to history, the standpoint from which one truly interprets history and therefore has the possibility of being relevantly committed to the service of God in history now.

5. To speak of commitment to the service of God through Jesus Christ is to approach the question of conversion. To claim finality for Christ in this sense is to imply a summons to men to forsake other claims to ultimate loyalty and to be converted to him. This is the point at which the claim to finality becomes actual and threatening. It is the point at which the charge of arrogance which is often levelled against a claim for the finality of Jesus becomes most insistent. It is also, as we shall see, the point at which the detailed questions we have discussed assume their sharpest form – the question of continuity or discontinuity between the Gospel and other religions; the question of the place of the Church in the things for which finality is claimed, and the relation of the claim for finality to the question of action in the secular world. A discussion of the meaning of the Christian claim for the finality of Jesus cannot be closed without treating the question of conversion.

NOTES

1. Tillich, *Christianity and the Encounter of the World Religions*, p. 58.

2. *Ibid.*, p. 74.

3. Alan Richardson.

4. *Ecumenical Review* XVIII (1) (1966), pp. 1–26.

V

Conversion

Conversion is not a popular word. There are many among the most sensitive spirits who deplore the effort to persuade a person to change his religious allegiance. Part of this feeling is due to the suspicion that unworthy means have often been used to bring about this change. It is rightly felt that there is something contemptible about any use of material means to persuade or coerce people into changing their religious affiliation, and a person who resists such tactics will always earn the approval of decent men. But even if all unworthy means of persuasion are eliminated (and it must be sadly confessed that they have not been eliminated), it is still felt by many that there is something intrinsically undesirable about any attempt to win converts for one's own religious group. Proselytism – the enterprise of gaining proselytes for one's own faith – is almost universally condemned, though there is little clarity about what is exactly the difference between 'proselytism' and 'evangelism'; at the end of many discussions of the matter one is inclined to conclude that the only workable distinction is that evangelism is what we do and proselytism is what others do.

The traditional Hindu position on the matter of conversion is well known. 'Reality is one; the sages call it by many names.' The sincere Hindu at his best will advise the Christian or Muslim to strive to become a better Christian, a better Muslim, rather than urging him to become a Hindu. This attitude is based upon the fundamental belief that the reality to which different religions give different names is in fact the same, and that – except in unusual cases – it is better to seek that reality along the path for which one's religious and cultural training has prepared one.

But a similar position is now very common also in the western world. It is normal now, in the most influential circles – both Catholic and Protestant – to stress the role of missionaries in technical development, and to deprecate any suggestion that their primary purpose is to win converts from other faiths to the Christian Church. Many enthusiastic churchmen in the West will strongly deplore such an effort and will insist that there are much more important tasks than that of persuading Hindus or Muslims to become Christians.

If one tries to state precisely the reasons for this attitude, something like the following may be suggested as a provisional statement:

(*a*) The Hindu view that the reality behind all religions is the same is – consciously or otherwise – very commonly at the bottom of this attitude.

(*b*) There is, secondly, the conviction that religion is primarily a matter of inward faith, and that to seek the aggrandisement of a religious society or institution is unworthy of the highest religion. Cannot the Hindu become a sincere follower of Jesus Christ without breaking his solidarity with his own people by baptism? Are there not, in fact, many examples of such devout and sincere believers outside of the Church – believers whose Christian faith is much more real than that of many church members?

(c) Thirdly, there is the conviction that there are more important issues in the world to day than those involved in a conversion, say, from Hinduism to Christianity. From the point of view of the reign of God, of the doing of God's will in the world, is it not much more important to see that men take the right positions on the great issues of war and peace, of social justice, of racial unity, of the sanctity of marriage and similar issues, than that they should be persuaded to change their allegiance from some other faith to the Christian Church?

It will be seen that these three convictions touch exactly the main points which we have had to discuss in the course of the preceding chapters. All the issues discussed in the first three chapters come to a sharp focus at this point of conversion; at this point they become not academic questions but very practical and indeed painful ones. Thus:

(a) The question of continuity and discontinuity between the Christian faith and other faiths becomes a burning question at this point. Conversion implies a real discontinuity. It implies a negative judgment of a very sharp kind upon the faith which the convert leaves. Whatever he may ultimately come to think, at that moment his act implies that that faith is not a way to God – at least for him.

(*b*) The question of the sense in which the Church belongs to those things for which finality is claimed becomes a burning question at the point of conversion. At the moment when he accepts baptism and joins the Church, the convert confesses, in effect, not only that he believes in the finality of the revelation of God in Jesus Christ, but also in the necessity of this community as part of the response to that revelation.

(*c*) The question of the relation of Christ to the secular history of mankind comes to a focus at the point of conversion. Conversion has always an ethical content; it involves not only joining a new community but also accepting a new pattern of conduct. Conversion implies that the convert accepts this new pattern of conduct as that which is relevant for the doing of God's will and the fulfilment of his reign at this particular juncture of world history.

Every conversion is a particular event shaped by the experience of the convert and by the life of the Church as it is at that place and time. The Church may be so corrupt that the judgment upon the other faith is a false judgment, the community is a self-regarding and unredemptive community, and the pattern of conduct is largely irrelevant to the real purposes of God at that moment of history. What is said about conversion, therefore, must be subjected to the judgment of the revelation itself. Like everything else in the life of the Church, it must submit to the standard of Scripture. In the present chapter, therefore, we shall look at what conversion means in the New Testament, bearing in mind the three points which have been referred to. We shall ask – seeking always to answer the question in the light of the revelation of God in Jesus Christ – what kind of conversion is the proper response to this revelation? and – more precisely – what are the mutual relations within the total fact of conversion of the three elements: inward religious experience, commitment to a community, and acceptance of a pattern of conduct?

According to all the four Gospels, the ministry of Jesus was introduced by the appearance of John the Baptist with his summons to Israel to radical repentance and conversion. By his own baptism, Jesus made himself one with this call to corporate repentance, and in this act his own ministry was inaugurated. Moreover when, at a later stage, he was challenged as to the source of his authority, he used the baptism of John as the test by which it could be determined whether or not a man was capable of recognizing true authority (Mark 11.27 ff.). And according to the Fourth Gospel, Jesus told another of the Jewish elders that without the baptism of water and the Spirit it is impossible to see the Kingdom of God, which is perhaps another way of saying the same thing. John's call to conversion, signalized by the act of baptism, was fundamental for the ministry of Jesus.

This baptism and preaching of John was in the line of the prophetic preaching. In John's call to repentance, and in the outward sign by which it was accompanied, men recognized the authentic marks of the prophet; at the very heart of the prophetic word there had always been the call to return to the Lord, to re-turn, to be converted. Three things may be noted about this call as it is found in the prophets and in John:

(*a*) It is a call addressed to God's people as a whole, but this by no means excludes the call to the individual to be converted. This is extremely clear in the case of John, whose mission was to the nation but who baptized individuals.

(*b*) It is a call to concrete obedience here and now in the context of the actual issues of the day. Neither the teaching of the Old Testament prophets, nor that of John, provides any basis for the view of conversion which is very common among Christians, namely that conversion is some sort of purely inward and spiritual experience which is later followed by a distinct and different decision to act in certain ways. The idea that one is first converted, and then looks round to see what one should do as a consequence, finds no basis in Scripture. And yet this idea (perhaps not usually expressed so crudely) is very common. In a paper read to the Central Committee of the World Council of Churches in 1965 the statement was made that conversion has to be followed 'by a later diaconical decision based on other supplementary theological principles'. The same idea has been expressed in recent years by the formula of two conversions: one from the world to Christ, and the second from Christ to the world. All such language arises from the attempt to correct a false conception of conversion, namely the idea that conversion is a purely inward experience which does not intrinsically and of itself involve certain decisions about conduct. A careful study of the biblical use of the language of conversion, of returning to the Lord, will show that, on the contrary, it is always in the context of concrete decisions at the given historical moment.

This is a very important practical issue, in view of the fact that one of the most tragic divisions in the Body of Christ today is between those who place their whole emphasis upon the conversion of the individual and those who place their emphasis upon radical social and political action. To heal this wound is one of the most pressing tasks of today. It can only be done by returning to the biblical sources of the very word 'conversion'.

The chapter on 'Conversion and Social Transformation' by Emilio Castro, written in preparation for the World Conference on Church and Society, includes a very clear refutation of the 'two conversions' model. Yet even in this treatment of the matter there seems to be a remnant of the wrong idea of conversion when the example of the liberation of the children of Israel from Egypt is used to illustrate the relation between social factors and the possibility of conversion. 'Liberty was a basic requisite for worship. Could God work among slaves? Undoubtedly he could, but slavery is not what he willed for his children. Liberty makes genuine worship possible. The fact is completed when, in the book of Joshua, after the conquest of Canaan, the people are faced with this choice: "Choose you this day whom you will serve." Liberty makes conversion possible.'[1] But surely this is to fall back into the wrong conception of conversion as a purely religious pheno-

menon separated from its social context. The real
conversion surely came earlier. Moses could not have
led the people out of Egypt unless they had (with whatever doubts and backslidings) believed his word that he
was sent from the Lord, and that it was the Lord's
purpose thus to deliver them. The real moment of conversion was when Moses and Aaron first gathered the
people together in Egypt and 'spoke all the words which
the Lord had spoken to Moses and did the signs in the
sight of the people. And the people believed . . . and
bowed their heads and worshipped' (Exodus 4.30–31).
From that time onwards (not without innumerable
lapses into unbelief) the people were facing the other
way; they were no longer living with their faces to
the ground; they were facing the Promised Land, and
were committed to all the dangers and labour of the
exodus and the Long March. That was the conversion
– the turning which involved in itself everything that
was to follow, even though it would take time to learn
all that was involved.

(*c*) The call to conversion is, from one point of view,
a call back, a re-call to re-turn. The word of Moses and
Aaron to the children of Israel was a word from 'the
God of your fathers, of Abraham and Isaac and Jacob'.
The call to return in the mouth of the great prophets
was a call to return to the covenant given on Sinai.
And yet it is always a call to the future. The God who
appears to Moses gives as his only name: I will be who
I will be. The Lord who calls is he who goes before in
the pillar of cloud and fire. The call to return as sounded
by the prophets is in the context of the coming 'day

of the Lord'. It faces the future. And this is supremely true of the message of John the Baptist. He is the one who cries: Prepare the way of the Lord. His message is of one who is coming.

The preaching of Jesus follows directly upon that of John. It is a call to repent (to be converted) in view of the coming reign of God. The time is fulfilled; the reign of God is at hand; repent and believe the good news. The repentance, the conversion, is in view of the Good News. It is as though someone were to say: the person you are waiting for is coming, but you cannot see him unless you turn round and look the other way. Conversion, then, means being turned round in order to recognize and participate in the dawning reality of God's reign. But this inward turning immediately and intrinsically involves both a pattern of conduct and a visible companionship. It involves membership in a community and a decision to act in certain ways.

1. It involves a visible community. At the very beginning of the story we find Jesus going out and finding certain men to join him in his movement. The names of the first apostles appear almost at the beginning of the story. There is not merely a broadcast invitation to conversion, to which those interested may attend; there is also a laying hold of certain individuals with a summons to leave their present commitments and be wholly committed to him. Peter and Andrew were facing one way; Jesus turns them round to face the other way and to be henceforth committed to his immediate and constant companionship. A visible community takes shape by his deliberate, individual and

concrete acts of calling. What happened at the beginning is vividly summarized in the word ascribed to Jesus by the Fourth Evangelist: 'You did not choose me; I chose you and appointed you to go and bear fruit'. Conversion is a work of God. It is the summoning of men and women into a visible fellowship with a view to the carrying out of God's will in the world.

At this point we come to a very important issue. It has often been pointed out that it was significant that Jesus chose twelve men – the number of the tribes of Israel. This is a representative number. He did not simply invite anyone who cared to join. He chose twelve. The twelve in some sense represent Israel; but in what sense? They are the *pars pro toto*, the part which represents the whole. But in what sense do they represent the whole? What is the force of the *pro*? Does this little preposition mean 'with a view to', or 'instead of'? Some modern theologians appear to adopt the latter meaning. They seem to teach that the Church is the *pars pro toto* in the sense that the rest of the world is already adequately represented by the Church and needs no conversion. Or is the Church the *pars pro toto* in the sense that it is sent in order that the rest of the world may be converted? That certainly seems to be the sense implied in the story of the calling of the first apostles, who are promised that they will become fishers of men. But there is also evidence in the Bible to suggest that the other meaning is not altogether excluded. A visible fellowship is central to God's plan of salvation in Christ; but God's plan of salvation is not limited to the visible fellowship.

D

2. Conversion involves a pattern of conduct. St Matthew's Gospel goes almost straight on from the first announcement of the kingdom and call to conversion to the Sermon on the Mount. Here is grouped together a representative body of Jesus' teaching. It is not a new law, but it is a vivid description of the kind of conduct which will be involved in accepting the good news of the coming reign of God. To be converted is to be turned round so as to recognize and participate in this coming reign, and this is what participation will mean.

Thus the three elements to which we have referred are present from the beginning as intrinsic elements in the total fact of conversion: an inward turning of the heart and mind, commitment to a visible fellowship, and commitment to a kind of conduct. Almost from the beginning, as we shall see, the relation between these three becomes a matter of acute debate.

When we move from the first preaching of Jesus to the preaching of the apostles after Pentecost we find that the same elements are present. There is a call to radical conversion, which carries with it membership in a visible fellowship and commitment to a way of behaviour.

Even though the Gospel narratives are largely within Judaism, there is always the consciousness of the wider horizon. We remember such words as 'Many will come from the East and the West and sit down in the kingdom', and the great saying in the context of the visit of the Greek enquirers: 'I, if I am lifted up, will draw all men unto myself.' The narrative of Acts seems to

make it absolutely clear that this drawing is not a sort
of painless or unconscious process. It is not simply
that the world has been saved even though it does not
know it. The character of Christ's action is the same
throughout. It is a call for radical repentance, conversion and baptism. When the people heard the first
Christian preaching they were cut to the heart and said
to Peter: 'What shall we do?' Peter said, 'Repent, be
baptized every one of you in the name of Jesus Christ
for the forgiveness of your sins and you shall receive
the Holy Spirit. The promise is to you and your children and to all that are afar off, every one whom the
Lord calls.' That does not mean, however, that the
promise does not need to be accepted. There is an
R.S.V.P. on this card. 'And those who received the
word were baptized and there were added that day
three thousand souls, and they devoted themselves
to the apostles' teaching and fellowship, to the breaking of the bread and the prayers.' This, at the beginning
of Acts, corresponds to what we have seen at the beginning of Mark. It is the call to radical conversion and
commitment, and to becoming part of a visible fellowship.

Similar language is used when we find the apostles
beginning to talk to the gentiles, to the pagans outside of Judaism. When the pagan people of Lystra
think that Paul and Barnabas are gods and try to offer
sacrifice, Paul cries out to them: 'Why are you doing
this? We are men like you and bring you good news
that you should turn from these vain things to the living God who made the heaven and the earth and the

3913

sea and all that is in them.' Again, in a very pregnant phrase, he addresses the Church in Thessalonica as those who have turned (been converted) from idols to serve the living and true God and to wait for his Son from heaven.

To sum up very briefly, the evidence of Acts is in line with the word at the close of St Luke's Gospel: 'Thus it is written that Christ should suffer, that he should rise from the dead, and that repentance and forgiveness of sin should be preached in his name to all nations.' The universality of Christ's lordship over all nations and over all creation is not, in the New Testament, a ground for leaving all the nations as they are. It is on the other hand exactly the ground for the Church's mission to preach repentance to every man and to all nations. The logic of the matter is most clearly set out in Romans 10.12 and the following verse: 'There is no distinction between Jew and Greek; the same Lord is Lord of all, and bestows his riches upon all who call upon him. For everyone who calls upon the name of the Lord will be saved.' This is a very complete statement on the universality of Christ's rule. The text goes on: 'How are men to call upon him if they do not believe? How are they to believe if they have never heard? And how are they to hear without a preacher? And how can men preach unless they are sent?' That is the logic of universality as St Paul interprets it.

This passage provides the transition to one of the most hotly debated of the issues which we have to discuss: does fidelity to Christ require us also to try to draw men into the fellowship of the visible Church? Is not God also active – and savingly active – in the world outside the Church? Does the Bible itself not make this plain? Is it not, therefore, much more important for us to co-operate with men of all faiths in doing the work of God in the world, than to try to draw men out of the world into the Church? Is there not here a clear choice for Christians between unselfish commitment to serving God in the world and a selfish desire to build up the Church as a separate body apart from the world?

Three things are to be noted about what Paul says in this passage. Firstly, there is a tremendous asser- tion of the universality of God's love. God's grace is not limited by any ecclesiastical barriers. 'There is no distinction between Jew and Greek; the same Lord is Lord of all, and bestows his riches upon all who call upon him.' Secondly, there is a radical insistence upon the freedom of God over against his own people. God's own people are those who are obstinately deaf, and it is the pagans who hear and understand. The two quotations from the Old Testament put this very sharply: 'I have been found by those who did not seek me; I have shown myself to those who did not ask for me'; but of Israel he says, 'All day long I have held out my hands to a disobedient and contrary people'. God is not the property of the ecclesiastical establishment; he is free – free to manifest himself to the pagan. And yet, thirdly, there is no question whatever about the need for repentance and faith. The passage as a whole makes it quite clear that the references are to the believing pagans. It is those who 'call upon the name of the Lord' who will be saved. Conscious belief, and explicit verbal confession of Jesus as Lord (Romans 10.9), are the conditions for salvation.

St Paul does not question the belief upon which all Hebrew faith depends, that God has in very truth chosen a people and set it apart for his service; there is a people of God, recognizable to eyes of faith as a visible historic community. But, argues the apostle, God has not therefore surrendered his freedom of action. The children of Abraham are God's people, but 'God is able of these stones to raise up children to Abraham' (Luke 3.8). Israel is the olive tree that God planted; but he can graft wild shoots into the tree and make them part of it, and can also break off the natural branches of the tree (Romans 11). God remains free and sovereign, and therefore the extension of his reign is not to be identified simply with the extension of the community which is called to be his people. The community which he has chosen and called is central to his purpose, but his purpose is not to be identified simply with the aggrandisement of the community. In what sense, then, is 'membership in the visible fellowship' integral to conversion? To put it in terms of the current debate: is it the best service to God's kingdom to draw men into visible membership of the Christian Church? Or, as it has been sharply put recently in India: 'Does a Hindu have to be baptized in order to belong to Christ?'

As is well known, the crucial battle (which lies behind Paul's words in Romans 10) was fought over the issue of the circumcision of the gentile converts. To many it seemed obvious that pagans who accepted the Gospel must fulfil the basic visible requirement for member-ship in the visible company of God's people; they must be circumcised. But in the end, as is well known, the decision went the other way. The churches in Corinth and Ephesus and Rome were not to be mere extensions of Judaean Christianity. The gentile converts were not to be Jewish *Assimilados*. And, as Roland Allen has pointed out in a vivid passage, a Jewish Christian who happened to attend a meeting for Christian worship in Corinth would probably have been profoundly shocked at something which would appear to him so appallingly pagan claiming to be the community of God's people. In spite of the shock, however, the deci-sion was made and adhered to that conversion to Christ did not mean – for the gentile – incorporation into the existing Jewish Church as it was before the gentile mission began.

But, in this context, two points have to be noticed:

1. The reason for which it was decided that gentile converts should not be circumcised was not any kind of doubt about the centrality of the community in God's saving purpose. The reason is very explicitly set forth in the relevant chapters of Acts and in St Paul's letters. It was because the Holy Spirit had been given to uncircumcised gentiles, and it was apparently impossible to deny this fact. The argument is set out in the speeches of Peter in Acts 11 and 15. 'God who knows the heart bore witness to them, giving them the Holy Spirit just as he did to us.' That was the new fact which required a new policy. The Epistle to the Ephesi-ans speaks of this new fact as something which was not

made known to the sons of men in other generations but has now been revealed to the apostles and prophets by the Holy Spirit (Ephesians 3.4–5). The gift of the Holy Spirit was something about which one could not be in doubt. It was a fact, and must be reckoned with. If the Holy Spirit was given to uncircumcised gentiles, then they were part of God's people.

2. The second point, however, which must be immediately noticed, is that those who had thus received the Holy Spirit were promptly incorporated into the community of the baptized. It would seem logical to argue that since Cornelius and his family were the recipients of the Spirit being both uncircumcised and unbaptized, neither circumcision nor baptism was necessary. In point of fact, however, the first thing Peter did was to baptize them. Thus, while there was no question of making the gentile converts mere extensions of Judaism, they were certainly incorporated into a visible and definite community. They were baptized and – presumably – incorporated into that fellowship which had its centre in the Lord's Table.

Thus, to sum up the present section of the argument, conversion does not mean *simply* being incorporated into the given community. Conversion is a fresh act of the Holy Spirit and may, therefore, carry as one of its consequences profound changes in the structure of the community. True conversion is a new birth from above, not a mere act of self-aggrandisement by the existing community. The coming in of the gentile converts profoundly changed the nature of the Christian community. Nevertheless conversion does involve incorporation into a community. The gentile converts were *not* asked to become Jewish Christians, but they *were* baptized. Robert di Nobili's Brahman converts in Madurai were not incorporated into the Portuguese mission station, but they were baptized and received to Holy Communion. If di Nobili's critics had not been successful in discrediting him, it could have happened that these converts would have profoundly changed the character of the Indian Christian community as we know it today. One could wish that it had been so. Nevertheless the wrong was not all on one side in that controversy. It was, no doubt, really shocking to the Christians in the Portuguese mission to see a sort of *apartheid* permitted within the Christian Church. The question: 'What elements of continuity are necessarily involved between the old community and the new convert?' is one on which there will always be room for debate.

This debate has become rather vigorous in India recently through the writings of Dr Kaj Baago of Bangalore. Looking at the foreign elements in Indian Christianity he has put the question: 'Must Buddhists, Hindus and Muslims become Christians in order to belong to Christ? Do they have to be incorporated in Church organizations which are utterly alien to their religious traditions? Do they have to call themselves Christians – a word which signifies a follower of the western religion? Should they necessarily adopt the Christian traditions, customs and rites which often have their root in western culture more than in the Gospel? Are all these things conditions for belonging to Christ?' To these questions Dr Baago obviously answers No. 'The Christian religion, to a large extent a product of the west, cannot and shall not become the religion of all nations and races. . . . The missionary task of today cannot, therefore, be to draw men out of their religions into another religion, but rather to leave Christianity (the organized Christian religion) and go inside Hinduism and Buddhism, accepting these religions as one's own in so far as they do not conflict with Christ, and regarding them as the presupposition, the background and the framework of the Christian gospel in Asia. . . . Jesus is not the monopoly of the Christians. . . . He is for all men; he is to be incarnated in all religions, not just in Christianity.'[2]

Dr Baago reaches his conclusion by loading the word 'Christian' with all the colonial baggage that it will carry. If the word 'Christian' means everything that has been perpetrated during the past two hundred and fifty years in Asia by persons professing the Christian religion, then we do not wish Hindus to become Christians. But it would be equally pertinent to put the question the other way round and ask: 'Can a Hindu who has been born again in Christ by the work of the Holy Spirit be content to remain without any visible solidarity with his fellow-believers?' The answer to that question is No. The New Testament knows nothing of a relationship with Christ which is purely mental and spiritual, unembodied in any of the structures of human relationship. And if it is an embodied relationship, obviously it is liable to be influenced by all the accidental – and potentially sinful – facts of human cultural and political life. Neither of these two questions takes us to the heart of the problem. True conversion involves *both* a new creation from above, which is not merely an act of extension of the existing community, and *also* a relationship with the existing community of believers. The real question is: What is the relation between these two? In the transmission of the Gospel, what are the essentials without which the Gospel is not truly communicated? How much of what we have received (*traditum*) belongs to the fundamental *tradendum*?

This is the question to which (in the context of the modern missionary movement) Roland Allen devoted his passionate, sometimes irritating but usually inescapable argument. Roland Allen, contrasting the missionary methods of the nineteenth century with those of St Paul, argued that modern misions had completely strayed from the true path. They had attempted to export to the peoples of the non-European world a whole mass of stuff which does not belong to the *tradendum*. If I understand him rightly, his contention was that the essential *tradenda* are: the Bible, the sacraments of Baptism and the Lord's Supper, and the apostolic ministry. (Unlike most of his followers, Allen was a High Churchman.) Allen, therefore, waged war against everything that had been confused with these essentials, everything that makes missions look like a piece of Western imperialism – the whole apparatus of a professional ministry, institutions, church buildings, church organizations, diocesan offices – everything from harmoniums to archdeacons.

Many missionaries wrestling with these problems have asked whether Allen was not over-simplifying. I think the question is fair. If we go back again to the New Testament we find that there is room for a great deal of debate. The famous decision recorded in Acts 15 did not merely include the negative, liberating provision about circumcision; it also included the statement that the following were necessary and were to be binding upon the gentile converts: 'that you abstain from what has been sacrificed to idols, from blood and from what is strangled and from unchastity'. That was the Jerusalem quadrilateral, but it has not remained operative. Even the Jerusalem fathers were not consistently radical. When we come to St Paul's letters we find a distinction made between what is the command of the Lord and what is personal judgment, and even in respect of some of the things which the apostle ascribes to the Lord, we have doubts today as to whether they belong to the essence of the *tradendum*. There was and there will remain room for debate. We may agree with Allen that modern missions have mixed up with the *tradendum* a lot that does not belong to it; but we may not be able to accept all the clear-cut lines that he draws. It is surely significant that for many decades the Roman authorities regarded the Christian Church as an extension of Judaism and treated it as such. It was by no means clear at once that this was not so. The conclusion which I would draw from this argument is something like the following.

1. There will always be, and there should be, a tension between that element of discontinuity which is

created by the fact of true conversion and the element of continuity without which there is no Christian Church. On the one hand every true conversion is a new creative event which – in principle – may call in question the existing life of the community. On the other hand, all conversion involves also commitment to the visible fellowship of those who belong to Christ. The relationship of the Christian with Christ can never be a purely mental and spiritual one; it is an embodied relationship and the body is – in principle – the whole body of believers. It is useless to try to remove the tension involved by trying to deny either side of it. The Church grows and justifies its claim to have the clue to history only by living with this tension.

2. The classic definition of the *tradendum* is given in what is said about the very first converts of the apostolic preaching: 'Those who received his word were baptized and they devoted themselves to the apostles' teaching and fellowship, to the breaking of bread and the prayers.' No doubt there is vast room for debate about the full implications of each of these phrases; nevertheless they point to that which is fundamental. If these things are not transmitted then the end of preaching has not been achieved. I would not say, with Allen, that all else is excluded; I would simply say that all else is subject to debate and decision in the Church from time to time. Whatever content has been loaded into the word 'Christian' through the centuries of sinful church history, the proper meaning of the word is: one who is baptized, who regularly shares in the Lord's Supper, who abides in the teaching

of the apostles through faithful study of the Scriptures, and in their fellowship through his participation in the common life of prayer and service. In that sense of the word, I would encourage a believing Hindu to become a Christian. I will not say to him: 'Become one of us, a Christian like me and follow all the habits and customs you see among the people called Christians.' Nor will I say to him: 'Remain a Hindu and worship Jesus in the context of Hindu faith and practice.' I would want to say rather: 'Be a Christian in the sense which I have defined, and let the Holy Spirit who has brought you to Christ teach us too what it means to be a Christian.'

In this discussion we have already approached the ethical aspect of conversion – the question of the pattern of conduct involved by conversion. We have seen that at every level of the biblical evidence conversion carries with it commitment to certain kinds of conduct. In the Gospels, conversion is a turning round which enables a man to believe in and to participate in the coming reign of God. In the previous chapter I said that to claim finality for Christ meant to claim that, through participation in the community which is committed to Christ as Lord one is enabled rightly to interpret God's work in history, and thereby rightly to commit oneself to constructive action in history. This claim comes to a point in the issue of conversion. Conversion to Christ, properly understood, is such a turning round that, in the fellowship of those similarly committed, one is enabled to act in history in a way that bears witness to and carries forward God's real purpose for the creation.

Our difficulty arises from the fact that the community which bears the name of Christ is constantly guilty of turning its back on God's purpose for the creation and concentrating upon the selfish enjoyment of its own privileges. Constantly it is guilty of blindness to the great issues of public life in which God's will is flouted and denied, while concentrating on relatively minor ethical issues in respect of which Christians try to keep their consciences clear and thereby enjoy a kind of false spiritual security. The ethical content of conversion at any place and time will be very much determined by the character of the Christian community. In such circumstances as I have described, conversion may for practical purposes be defined in terms of ethical decisions which have little relevance to the big issues of the time. At such times and places it may often happen that those who profess no faith in the Gospel may be serving God in the big battles of human life more effectively than Christians are. Such persons will be the instruments of God's judgment upon the Church, as the Bible in many passages teaches us. The Church has to be constantly open and sensitive to this judgment.

And yet conversion in the biblical sense is not simply conversion to a programme. Certainly conversion involves commitment to the doing of God's will in the world. But it is not just that; if it were we should have law but no Gospel. Conversion is something more radical than that. It involves the deepest possible kind of personal cleansing, forgiveness, reconciliation and renewal. It involves the replacement of alienation by a loving personal relationship, constantly renewed, between the self and the source of its being. But this blessed fact also provides the occasion for temptation; the accent can shift so exclusively to this aspect of what conversion means, that commitment to the work of God in the world becomes something secondary. Conversion comes to be thought of as 'being saved'. The accent falls on the privileges of membership in the saved community. The eschatological dimension of the biblical idea of salvation slips out of sight; one forgets that 'being saved' means being made a participant in the mighty saving work of God which is not complete until all things have been summed up in Christ. And in this context, where the Church is seen simply as the exclusive association of those who have been rescued from perdition, an anxious discussion about whether others too might not be saved becomes inevitable.

Surely the perspective is wrong. Conversion means being turned round so as to be by faith and in foretaste a participant in and an agent of God's reign. The proper question is not: Are there few that be saved? The question is: Who is doing the will of God? To speak of the finality of Christ is not, primarily, to speak of the fate of those who do not accept him as Lord; discussion often proceeds as if it were. It is to say that commitment to Christ in the fellowship of those who share the same commitment is the clue to a true participation in God's purpose for his whole creation. The privileges to which conversion is the gateway are not exclusive claims upon

God's grace; they are the privileges of those who have been chosen for special responsibility in the carrying out of God's blessed design. Their joy will be not that they are saved, but that God's name is hallowed, his will done and his reign perfected. There are many hints in the Bible which suggest that this saving purpose will extend beyond those who are its conscious agents. Indeed the metaphor of salt, used of the disciples, suggests that the Church has a function to the world which extends far beyond the boundaries of its own membership.

Conversion will always be wrongly understood unless it is remembered that the Church is the *pars pro toto*. God converts a man not only that he may be saved, but also that he may be the sign, earnest and instrument of God's total plan of salvation. There is therefore a tension involved in the very idea of conversion. It has been well stated by Dr Paul Löffler in a paper prepared for the World Council of Churches. Conversion, he writes, 'demands commitment of some – not for their own sake but for the salvation of all. Conversion has always this double dimension: as a call it is uttered to all nations, as a potential it concerns the destiny of all men. But as a realization here and now it singles out an exemplary few who begin to enter into the community of the Church. The temptation with conversion has often been to short-circuit this very eschatalogical tension, either by reserving it for the few who are saved, or by letting it be submerged in a universalism which does not recognize any form of definite commitment. Conversion bears the eschatological tension. It shares in the "already" in that it is a definite call to personal commitment to the visible but not limited corporate being of the Church in Christ. Conversion actually establishes a new relationship between God and man. Yet its fulfilment will be realized only through the consummation of all things. Conversion is a commitment to a companionship on the way. It lives towards the "not yet".[3]

The nineteenth century stressed one side of this tension. It tended to be obsessed by the thought that all those who had not made that personal commitment were everlastingly damned. Missions were a heroic struggle to stem that appalling avalanche. Our time is in danger of overstressing the other side of the tension, and losing all sense of the call to personal commitment in a general universalism. I cannot find anything in the New Testament to support what seems to be a widespread view today, namely that whereas it is tolerable to think of a few people being lost, it is intolerable to think of the majority of mankind being lost. Certainly this is not God's arithmetic according to the parables of Jesus. He is the one who cares for the unique individual, the last and least. I do not find in the New Testament a God who is impressed by majorities, or daunted by monster deputations. I do not find grounds in the New Testament for Dr Baago's view that because few Hindus or Muslims are converted to Christianity, therefore the idea of conversion must be abandoned.

We are not permitted to anticipate the last judgment. We do not know everything; we know a few things, but they are enough. God's call is addressed to all men; those who are converted are few. Those few are chosen not for themselves but for the sake of the doing of God's will, as witnesses and signs and agents of his saving purpose. If they forget this, they themselves will be rejected.

To claim finality for Jesus Christ is not to assert either that the majority of men will some day be Christians, or to assert that all others will be damned. It is to claim that commitment to him is the way in which men can become truly aligned to the ultimate end for which all things were made. The Church which believes this will not be afraid to address confidently to every generation and every people the call which it has received from him: Follow me.

NOTES

1. E. Castro, 'Conversion & Social Transformation', in: *Christian Social Ethics in a Changing World* (London and New York 1966), pp. 356–7.

2. Kaj Baago, 'The Post-Colonial Crisis of Missions', *International Review of Missions*, LV, No. 219, 1966, pp. 331–2.

3. *Study Encounter*, Vol. I, No. 2, pp. 98–99.

Bibliography

A. C. Bouquet, *Comparative Religion* (London: Cassell & Co., Ltd, 1961)

J. N. Farquhar, *The Crown of Hinduism* (London: Oxford University Press, 1913)

H. Kraemer, *The Christian Message in a Non-Christian World* (London: James Clarke, 1938)

   Religion and the Christian Faith (London: Lutterworth Press, 1956)

G. van der Leeuw, *Religion in Essence and Manifestation* (London: George Allen and Unwin, 1938)

A. T. van Leeuwen, *Christianity in World History* (London: Edinburgh House Press, 1964)

J. Moltmann, *Theology of Hope* (London: SCM Press and New York: Harper and Row, 1967)

L. Newbigin, *Honest Religion for Secular Man* (London: SCM Press and Philadelphia: Westminster Press, 1966)

R. Panikkar, *The Unknown Christ of Hindusim* (London: Darton, Longman and Todd, 1965)

E. J. Sharpe, *Not to Destroy but to Fulfil* (Uppsala, 1965)

The Authority of the Faith (Tambaram Series, Volume I) (International Missionary Conference, 1939)

The following books, which are immediately relevant to the issues discussed here, appeared too late to be discussed in the text:

W. Pannenberg, *Jesus – God and Man* (London: SCM Press and Philadelphia: Westminster Press, 1968)

M. M. Thomas, *The Acknowledged Christ of the Indian Renaissance* (London: SCM Press, 1969)

Index